Christmas, Easter, and Halloween

— Where Did They Come From?

Vance Ferrell

Harvestime Books

HB–1332
Christmas, Easter, and Halloween
  Where Did They Come From?
by Vance Ferrell
Published by Harvestime Books
Altamont, TN 37301 USA
Printed in the United States of America
Cover and Text Copyright © 2003

How thankful we can be for Jesus Christ, what He has done for us—and is doing right now. This book does not question the reality of our Lord and Saviour, the great work of redemption, or His soon coming in the clouds of heaven to redeem His people.

We do not question the truth of Christ's birth, but we would like to know where "Christmas" came from? And why is it celebrated on December 25? Who is "Santa Claus" and how did he get into Christmas?

We value the resurrection of Christ from the grave, but we would like to know the origin of "Easter," and why it is celebrated with bunny rabbits and colored eggs.

Then there is Halloween. Where did it come from? Why is it connected with witches, misshappen creatures, fires, and skeletons?

Additional copies: For additional copies of this book at remarkably low prices in boxful quantities, write to Harvestime Books, Altamont, TN 37301. When you write, ask for a copy of our "Missionary Book Order Sheet"; this contains low-cost boxful prices of this book and others, such as Great Controversy, Ministry of Healing, Bible Readings, etc.

Contents

Where Did Christmas Come From? 4

Historians Tell Us More
    about Christmas 17

Where Did Easter Come From? 44

Additional Historical Facts
    about Easter 51

Where Did Halloween Come From? 64

Additional Facts about Halloween 74

How to Come to Christ and
    Stay Close to Him 87

Entering a Deeper Walk with God 101

Source Index 124

Where Did Christmas Come From?

Yes, where did Christmas come from? It did not begin at the birth of Christ; it began earlier! The December 25 celebration had nothing to do with His birth. It is an interesting story; one I think you will be interested in.

WHEN WAS JESUS BORN?—It is well-know among Biblical scholars that Jesus was not born in December, because the shepherds were never out in the fields with their sheep at that time.

"There were in the same country shepherds abiding in the field, keeping watch over their flock by night."—Luke 2:8.

Shepherds always brought their sheep in from the mountainsides and field and corralled them not later than October 15, to protect them from the cold, rainy season that followed. (Also read Songs 2:11 and Ezra 10:9, 13.)

"It was an ancient custom among Jews of those days to send out their sheep to the fields and deserts about the Passover [early spring], and bring them home at commencement of the first rain. During the time they were out, the shepherds watched them night and day. As . . the first rain began early in the month of March, which answers to part of our October, we find that the sheep were kept out in the open country during the whole summer.

Where Did Christmas Come From?

"And, as these shepherds had not yet brought home their flocks [when Christ was born in Bethlehem], it is a presumptive argument that October had not yet commenced, and that, consequently, our Lord was not born on the 25th of December, when no flocks were out in the fields; nor could He have been born later than September, as the flocks were still in the fields by night. On this very ground the nativity in December should be given up. The feeding of the flocks by night in the fields is a chronological fact . . See the quotations from the Talmudists in Lightfoot."—*Adam Clarke, Commentary, Vol. 5, 370.*

The census of Caesar Augustus is mentioned in Luke 2:1-2, but historians are not certain when it was issued. But it is improbable that he would call for the citizens of the Roman Empire to return to their native homes, to be enrolled in the census in the middle of winter. Even his own armies avoided marching during the hazards of winter weather.

Many authorities believe that Christ was born in the spring of the year; but, in the wisdom of God, the date of Christ's birth has been hidden from us.

Why, then, does all the world celebrate the birth of Christ—not merely in December—but on a certain day in December?

We need to know (1) What is "Christmas?" (2) How did Christmas get into the Christian church? and (3) Why did it enter back in those early days? Here are answers to these questions:

WHAT IS "CHRISTMAS?"—The word, "Christmas," means "Mass of Christ" or, as it came to be shortened, "Christ-Mass." It came to the modern world from the Roman Catholic Church. Unfortunately, they did not get it from the Bible, but from paganism. Read this:

"Christmas was not among the earliest festivals of

the Church . . The first evidence of the feast is from Egypt. Pagan customs centering around the January calends [the pagan calendar] gravitated to Christmas."—*Catholic Encyclopedia, 1911 ed., "Christmas."*

Origen, an early Christian writer, said this about celebrating birthdays in the Bible:

"In the Scriptures, no one is recorded to have kept the feast or held a great banquet on his [Christ's] birthday. It is only sinners [like Pharaoh or Herod] who make great rejoicings over the day in which they were born into this world."—*Origen, quoted in Catholic Encyclopedia, 11th ed., "Natal Day."*

HOW DID CHRISTMAS GET INTO THE CHRISTIAN CHURCH?—In one brief paragraph, *the New Schaff-Herzog Encyclopedia of Religious Knowledge* tells us how the December 25 holiday entered the Christian church:

"How much the date of the festival depended upon the pagan *Brumalia* [The December 25 celebration], following the *Saturnalia* [an eight-day December 17-24 festival preceding it], and celebrating the shortest day of the year and the 'new sun' . . cannot be accurately determined. The pagan *Saturnalia* and *Brumalia* were too deeply entrenched in popular custom to be set aside by Christian influence . . The pagan festival with its riot and merrymaking was so popular that Christians were glad of an excuse to continue its celebration with little change in spirit and in manner. Christian preachers of the West and the Near East protested against the unseemly frivolity with which Christ's birthday was celebrated, while Christians of Mesopotamia accused their Western brethren of idolatry and sun worship for adopting as Christian this pagan festival."—*New Schaff-Herzog Encyclopedia of Religious Knowledge, "Christmas."*

Church leaders adopted a pagan holiday, in spite of

Where Did Christmas Come From?

the protests of some godly local pastors. It was considered idolatry to do this, since it was nothing more than a heathen day of worship. In addition, the day for this worship had been selected in honor of Mithra, the sun god. December 25 was dedicated to the keeping of his birthday. Therefore sincere Christians considered it to be a form of sun worship. The sun had reached its lowest angle in the sky on December 21 (the winter solstice), and the 25th was the first observable day in which it began rising in the noon sky. So December 25 had, for centuries, been celebrated as the "birth of the sun god."

But, back in those earlier centuries, earnest believers recognized that Christians dare not accept pagan practices or pagan holidays. These heathen customs are not found in the Bible as being used by Christians, so they ought to be shunned by conscientious Christians.

The Roman world was essentially pagan. Many converts to Christianity had come to enjoy those festivities and did not want to forsake them after baptism into the Christian church.

But when half-converted church members rose to positions of leadership in the Church, they made policy changes in agreement with contemporary heathen customs. And that is how we got Christmas.

"A feast was established in memory of this event [Christ's birth] in the fourth century. In the fifth century the Western Church ordered it to be celebrated forever on the day of the old Roman feast of the birth of Sol [the Latin word for 'sun'], as no certain knowledge of the day of Christ's birth existed."—*Encyclopedia Americana* (1944 edition), "Christmas."

If the Bible contained no certain knowledge of when Christ was born, then we should not try to select a definite day on which to worship Him. Instead, **we should remain with the only weekly worship day God ever gave us, the seventh-day Sabbath (Genesis 2:1-3, Exodus 20:8-11).**

The above quotation spoke about a pagan feast back then, in honor of the yearly birth of *Sol*. That word means "sun" in Latin and was another name for Mithra, the sun god. A strong controversy arose in the Christian church over this apostasy by Western church leaders:

"Certain Latins, as early as [A.D.] 354, may have transferred the birthday from January 6th to December 25, which was then a Mithraic feast . . or birthday of the unconquered sun . . The Syrians and Armenians accused the Romans of sun worship and idolatry."—Encyclopedia Britannica, 1946 ed.

It was clearly understood by the faithful Christians that this pagan holiday should not be adopted as the memorial day of the birth of Christ.

HOW DID MITHRA WORSHIP BRING THESE THINGS INTO THE CHRISTIAN CHURCH?—In order to understand how and why Christmas came into the Christian church back in those early centuries, **we need to understand the tremendous influence of pagan Mithraism in the first few centuries after the time of Christ—and how Christian leaders decided to adopt the customs of paganism in order to win the battle against it.**

The following information is vital and comes from an earlier study by the present writer:

THE PLANETARY WEEK—The various days of the week were, in ancient times, called *the first day, second day, etc.;* for these were their Biblical names. But about the time of Christ they were given new names. The non-Christians began calling them *the Day of the Sun,*

Where Did Christmas Come From?

the Day of the Moon, etc., in honor of different heavenly bodies. ***This was known by the pagans as the "planetary week."***

Each day was ruled over by a different god; but the most important of all gods was given the rule of the first day of the week, with the idea in mind that the first is always more important than that which follows it. The most important of all the heathen gods was given the rule over the first of the seven days. ***It was his day, the day of the Sun. And Mithra, the Sun god was worshiped each week on his day, the Sun day.***

Now, although these names for the days of the week were new, the day devoted to the Sun god was not new. The worship of the sun arose from a devotion to that most powerful of natural objects. It was one of the most ancient forms of worship and is represented by solar-disk images found on nearly every continent of our world.

"Sun worship was the earliest idolatry."—*A.R. Fausset, Bible Dictionary, page 666.*

The Arabians appear to have worshiped it directly without using any statue or symbol *(Job 31:26-27)*. Abraham was called out of all this when he went to the promised land. *Ra* was the Sun god of Egypt; and *On* (*Heliopolis*, which means "city of the sun" in Greek) was the center of Egyptian Sun worship *(see the Hebrew of Jer 43:13)*.

Entering Canaan under Joshua, the Hebrews again encountered Sun worship. *Baal* of the Phoenicians, *Molech* or *Milcom* of the Ammonites, *Hadad* of the Syrians, and later the Persian *Mitras* or *Mithra*.

Shemesh was an especially important Sun god in the Middle East. Later, in Egypt, *Aton* was the name of the god of the Sun Disk. The temple at *Baalbek* was dedicated to Sun worship.

By associating with Sun worshipers, the Israelites

frequently practiced it themselves (Lev 26:30, Isa 17:8). King Manasseh practiced direct Sun worship (2 Kgs 21:3, 5). Josiah destroyed the chariots that were dedicated to the Sun and worship processions (2 Kgs 23:5, 11-12). Sun altars and incense were burned on the housetops for the sun (Zeph 1:5). And Ezekiel beheld the "greatest abomination": direct Sun worship at the entry way to the temple of the true God. This was done by facing eastward to the rising sun (Eze 8:16-17).

MITHRA AND THE DAY OF THE SUN—All during those earlier centuries, there was no particular day that was used for heathen worship of the Sun god. But then, about the time of Christ, or a little before, the various days of the week were dedicated to specific pagan celestial gods—dies Solis—the day of the Sun, dies Lunae— the day of the Moon, and so on.

The sacred day of the Jews and Christians was the memorial of Creation—the true Sabbath—the seventh-day—the only weekly Sabbath given in the Bible. But, in marked contrast, the sacred day of paganism was the memorial of the Sun god—the first day of the week. His day was called "the Venerable Day of the Sun."

Sundaykeeping never occurred in the Old or New Testaments, nor was it commanded. In the time of Christ and the Apostles, the official religion of the Roman government did not have a sacred day, but gradually Sundaykeeping began to become common among the non-Christian people of the empire.

The planetary week, each day named after a different planet in the sky, played a very important part in the worship of the sun. By the time of Christ, Sun worship was most powerfully represented in Mithraism. Now, Mithra (also called Mithras) was originally an ancient god of Iran, and for centuries had been worshiped as the

Where Did Christmas Come From?   11

*god of strength and war by the descendants of the Persians. But, **by the first century A.D., Mithra had been transformed, oddly enough, into the leading Sun god—and foremost pagan god of any kind—throughout the Western civilized world.** The Romans often called him by a new name, Sol Invictus, "the Invincible Sun."*

*During the early centuries of the Christian Era, **Mithra was the greatest pagan rival of Christianity.** And this was not without a carefully developed plan; for **Satan had arranged that Mithraism would closely approximate, in several ways, the only true religion in the world—Christianity.** It had such similar features as a dying-rising Saviour, a special religious supper, a special holy day out of the weekly seven—the Sun Day, and baptism of converts to the faith by having blood from a slaughtered bull sprinkled upon them. It counterfeited the religion of the true God more cleverly than any other religion up to that time in history.*

Gradually, large numbers of non-Christians began observing Sunday as a holy day in honor of Mithra. He was especially adored by the Roman soldiers; for his worship included athletic feats of skill and "war-like manliness."

*Gradually, the worship of the Invincible Sun became even more popular and widespread among the Roman Empire. Then, about 200 years after the last book of the Bible had been penned, Emperor Aurelian (A.D. 270-275) whose mother was a priestess of the Sun, made this solar cult the official religion of the empire. His biographer, Flavius Vopiscus, says that the priests of the Temple of the Sun at Rome were called **pontiffs**. They were priests of their dying-rising Saviour, Mithra, and vicegerents in religious matters next to him.*

According to historical records, by this time (the

middle of the second century) worldly Christians in Alexandria and Rome, in order to be better accepted by their pagan neighbors, began keeping Sunday. "Lord Mithra" was a favorite name given him by his pagan worshipers; and they called his day "the Lord's Day."

The Christians in Alexandria and Rome, anxious to also copycat this aspect of paganism, began calling Sunday *"the Lord's Day,"* claiming that Sunday was the day mentioned in Revelation 1:10, even though it was obvious that this verse said nothing about Sunday.

In reality, when he spoke of the "Lord's day" in Revelation 1:10, the Apostle John meant that he saw Christ on the Bible Sabbath; for Christ had earlier said that He was "Lord of the Sabbath" (Matt 12:8, Mark 2:28). The terms, "Lord's day" and "day of the Lord," were repeatedly used in the Bible in describing the seventh-day Sabbath. It is the day unto the Lord (Ex 16:23, 25; 31:15; 35:2). It is the day of the Lord (Ex 20:10, Deut 5:14, Lev 23:3). It is the Lord's holy day (Isa 58:13). It is the day blessed and hallowed by the Lord (Gen 2:3). God had called it "My holy day" (Isa 58:13).

Sun worship continued to be the official religion of the empire until Constantine I defeated Licinius in 323, after which it was replaced by Romanized Christianity.

In every historical incident that the present writer can locate, the only Christian leaders advocating Sundaykeeping prior to A.D. 400—were the Christian philosophers at Alexandria and the Christian bishops in the city of Rome.

Along about this time, a youngster was growing up that was destined to powerfully affect the Christian world for all time to come—a boy named Constantine.

CONSTANTINE AND A STATE CHURCH—On the retirement of Emperor Diocletian in A.D. 305, it was an

Where Did Christmas Come From?

uphill fight among several men for the coveted title of Emperor. Fighting continued on and off, from 305 till 323. But out of it, Constantine emerged as the sole ruler of the vast Roman Empire. The crucial battle occurred just north of Rome in October of 312. Just afterward, by the *Edict of Milan*, Constantine gave Christianity full legal equality with every other religion in the empire. More favors to the church soon followed.

Then, on March 7, 321, the first national Sunday Law in history was decreed. This was the first "blue law" to be issued by a civil government. Here is the text of Constantine's Sunday Law Decree:

"*Let all judges and townspeople and occupations of all trades rest on **the Venerable Day of the Sun** [Sunday]; nevertheless, let those who are situated in the rural districts freely and with full liberty attend to the cultivation of the fields, because it frequently happens that no other day may be so fitting for ploughing grains, of trenching vineyards, lest at the time the advantage of the moment granted by the provision of heaven be lost. Given on the Nones [seventh] of March, Crispus and Constantine being consuls, each of them, for the second time.*"—*The Code of Justinian, Book 111, title 12, law 3.*

Five additional Sunday Laws were to be issued by Constantine, within a very few years, to strengthen this, his basic one.

It is to be observed that Constantine's Sunday Law was just that—a Sunday Law—and nothing more. It was a Sunday law that both Mithraists and compromising Christians could easily accept. **In that law, Christianity is never mentioned.** The day is called **"the Venerable Day of the Sun"** *(venarabili die solis)*. **This was the mystical name for the Day of Mithra, the Sun god.** Both the heathen and the Christians well-knew this. It is a historical fact that, when Constantine issued that first imperial Sunday edict of 321, enforcing the observance of Sunday by the people of the Roman Empire—he was still a worshiper of *Sol Invictus*, "the Invincible Sun," as well as being the *Pontifix Maximus* (supreme pagan pontiff or priest) of Roman heathen worship as the state religion.

Constantine intended that the law be a political means of uniting all contending religions into one giant compromising conglomerate: the Christian church. He believed that this would make the empire stronger and better able to defend itself against the marauding northern tribes. **But Christian leaders in Rome saw it as a great victory for the authority of the Roman Bishop (later given the title of "pope") over all other Christian congregations. And that is what happened.**

CHURCH ENFORCEMENT—The Roman bishop had encouraged Constantine to enact that law. Eusebius, bishop of Caesarea (270-338), generally considered to be Constantine's outstanding flatterer in the church, made this remarkable statement:

"All things whatsoever it was duty to do on the [seventh day] Sabbath, these we [the church] have transferred to the Lord's day [Sunday]."—*Commentary on the Psalms,* in Migne, *Patrologia Graeca,* Vol. 23, Col. 1171.

Commenting on this heaven-daring statement, one historical writer made this comment:

"Not a single testimony of the Scriptures was produced in proof of the new doctrine. **Eusebius himself unwittingly acknowledges its falsity and points to the real authors of change.** 'All things,' he says, 'whatever that it was duty to do on the Sabbath, these we have transferred to the Lord's day.' But the Sunday argument, groundless as it was, served to

Where Did Christmas Come From?   15

embolden men in trampling upon the Sabbath of the Lord. All who desired to be honored by the world accepted the popular festival."—Great Controversy, 574.

This was the beginning of something new and ominous within the Christian church. *Rome, itself, the capital of the mammoth empire, was more licentious, dissipated, and political than any other city. The Christian leaders in that city were more liberal and corrupt than Christian leaders elsewhere. Gripped by a concern to meet the world's standard and dabble in the power politics of the empire, the Roman bishop had Constantine convene church councils so the apostasy could spread outward to other Christian churches.*

In A.D. 325, the Council of Nicaea met; at which time the church leaders decreed that all must honor the resurrection of Christ by keeping the pagan Easter festival, but only on a certain Sunday of each year. *Immediately, following this ruling, Constantine issued an imperial order, commanding all Christians everywhere to obey the decrees of that council.* **Church and State had united; and, whenever in history this has happened, persecution of religious dissenters has eventually followed.** *Trouble was ahead for the people of God.*

PERSECUTION BEGINS—*From A.D. 350, onward, the persecution of Christians by their fellow Christians began.*

In order to placate church and government authorities, there were those who attempted to keep both days—Sabbath as well as Sunday holy—thus endeavoring to obey God as well as man; for religious persecution against non-observance of Sunday was growing stronger.

For this reason, Sozomen, a church historian of that time, told us this:

"[Many Christians] were assembling together on the

Sabbath as well as on the first day of the week, which custom is never observed at Rome or at Alexandria."— Sozomen, quoted in Ecclesiastical History, book 7, chapter 19; now in A Select Library of Nicene and Post-Nicene Fathers, second series, Vol. 2 (Luke 16:13, Acts 5:39).

Even at this late date, Rome and Alexandria continued to be the only bulwarks of strict Sundaykeeping.

The keeping of both days might seem a practical solution, but it wasn't. The seventh-day Sabbath was the divinely ordained day for the worship of the Creator. God had never changed it. The Sun day was a man-made institution of worship in honor of a pagan god. **To obey both was impossible** *(Matt. 6:24).*

This was exactly the problem the three Hebrew worthies faced at Dura (Read Daniel 3.) **Those three men were not, at that time, forbidden to worship the true God. They need only bow down, that day, with others in an appearance of worship to the false. But, of course, to do so would show an acceptance of heathen worship.**

And this they could not do. **They would rather die first. They would rather lose their lives than lose something that many in our day consider to be of little value— the Sabbath of the Fourth Commandment given by the God of Heaven Himself. Thus it was that Christmas—the birthday of the Sun god—and Sunday sacredness both came into the Christian church; because early church leaders in Rome and Alexandria, working with government leaders, wanted to unite Christianity with Mithraism—by requiring Mithraic practices in the worship of Christ.**

Gradually, more and more Sabbathkeepers were slain until, by the eleventh century, there were only a few people left who kept the Bible Sabbath.

Historians Tell Us More about Christmas

Historians, who have spent years studying this, explain how Christmas got its date and where Santa Claus, mistletoe, and other Christmas legends came from.

(If this chapter is a little deep, skip over to the next one, on page 44.)

DATE OF CHRIST'S BIRTH NOT KNOWN—"The supposed anniversary of the birth of Jesus Christ, occurring on Dec. 25: No sufficient data .. exists, for the determination of the month or the day of the event .. There is no historical evidence that our Lord's birthday was celebrated during the apostolic or early post-apostolic times.

"The uncertainty that existed at the beginning of the third century in the minds of Hippolytus and others—Hippolytus earlier favored Jan. 2; Clement of Alexandria (Strom., i. 21), "the 25th of Pachon" [May 20]; while others, according to Clement, fixed upon Apr, 18 or 19 and Mar. 28—proves that no Christmas festival had been established much before the middle of the century. Jan. 6 was earlier fixed upon as the date of the baptism or spiritual birth of Christ, and the feast of Epiphany .. was celebrated by the Basilidian Gnostics in the second century .. and by Catholic Christians by about the beginning of the fourth century.

"The earliest record of the recognition of Dec. 25 as a church festival is in the Philocalian Calendar [although copied in 354, represented Roman practice in 336]."—Newman, A.H., "Christmas," New Scaff-Herzog Encyclopedia of Religious Knowledge, Vol. 3, 47.

THEY WERE NOT CERTAIN WHAT DATE TO SELECT—"Uncertainty about Jesus' birthday in the early third century is reflected in a disputed passage of the presbyter Hippolytus, who was banished to Sarinia by Maximinus in 235, and in an authentic statement of Clement of Alexandria. While the former favored January second, the learned Clement of Alexandria enumerates several dates given by the Alexandrian chronographers, notably the twenty-fifth of the Egyptian month, Pachon (May twentieth), in the twenty-eighth year of Augustus and the twenty-fourth or twenty-fifth of Pharmuthi (April eighteenth or nineteenth) of the year A.D. 1, although he favored May twentieth. This shows that no Church festival, in honor of the day, was established before the middle of the third century. Origen, at that time in a sermon, denounced the idea of keeping Jesus' birthday like that of Pharaoh and said that only sinners such as Herod were so honored. Arnobius later similarly ridiculed giving birthdays to 'gods.' A Latin treatise, De pascha computus (of ca. 243), placed Jesus' birth on March twenty-first since that was the supposed day on which God created the Sun (Gen 1:14-19), thus typifying the 'Sun of righteousness' as Malachi 4:2 called the expected Messiah. A century before, Polycarp, martyred in Smyrna in 155, gave the same date for the birth and baptism placing it on a Wednesday because of the creation of the Sun on that day."—Walter Woodburn Hyde, Paganism to Christianity in the Roman Empire, 249-250.

Historians Tell Us More about Christmas

INITIALLY DIFFERENT DATES FOR MEMORIAL OF HIS BIRTH.—"The Oriental Christians kept the memorial of the Saviour's birth and of his baptism, on one and the same day, namely, the sixth day of January; and this day they called Epiphany. But the Occidental Christians always consecrated the 25th day of December to the memory of the Saviour's birth. For, what is reported of Julian I, the Roman bishop's transferring the memorial of Christ's birth from the 6th day of January to the 25th of December, appears to me very questionable."—John Laurence von Mosheim, D.D. Institutes of Ecclesiastical History, book 2, cent. 4, part 2, chap. 4, sec. 5 (Vol. I, 372-373). London: Longman & Co., 1841.

WHEN CHRISTMAS WAS FIRST OBSERVED—"The first footsteps we find of the observation of this day are in the second century, about the time of the emperor Commodus."—Charles Buck, A Theological Dictionary, "Christmas," Philadelphia: Crissy and Markley, copyright 1851, 71.

CHRISTMAS NOT AN OFFICIALLY ACCEPTED CHURCH DAY UNTIL THE FOURTH CENTURY.—"It is now generally granted that the day of the nativity was not observed as a feast in any part of the church, east or west, till some time in the fourth century. If any day had been earlier fixed upon as the Lord's birthday, it was not commemorated by any religious rites, nor is it mentioned by any writers."—Samuel J. Andrews, The Life of Our Lord Upon the Earth, New York: Charles Scribner's Sons, 1891, 17.

THE BIRTHDAY OF THE SUN WAS SELECTED—"The early Christians, who attributed to Christ not only the title (Kyrios) but also many other honors that the pagans paid to their 'divine' emperors, naturally felt inclined to honor the birth of the Saviour. In most places the commemoration of Christ's birth was included in the Feast of the Epiphany (Manifestations) on January 6, one of the oldest annual feasts.

"Soon after the end of the last great persecution, about the year 330, the Church of Rome definitely assigned December 25 for the celebration of the birth of Christ. For a while, many Eastern Churches continued to keep other dates, but toward the end of the fourth century the Roman custom became universal.

"No official reason has been handed down on ecclesiastical documents for the choice of this date. Consequently, various explanations have been given to justify the celebration of the Lord's nativity on this particular day. Some early Fathers and writers claimed that December 25 was the actual date of Christ's birth..

"It was expressly stated in Rome that the actual date of the Saviour's birth was unknown and that different traditions prevailed in different parts of the world.

"A second explanation was of theological-symbolic character. Since the Bible calls the Messiah the 'Sun of righteousness' (Malachi 4:2), it was argued that His birth had to coincide with the beginning of a new solar cycle, that is, He had to be born at the time of the winter solstice.. This explanation, though attractive in itself, depends on too many assumptions that cannot be proved and lacks any basis of historical certitude.

"There remains then this explanation, which is the most probable one, and held by most scholars in our time: the choice of December 25 is influenced by the fact that the Romans, from the time of Emperor Aurelian (275), had celebrated the feast of the sun god (Sol Invictus: the Unconquered Sun) on that day. December 25 was called the 'Birthday of the Sun,' and great pagan religious celebrations of the Mithras cult were held all through the empire. What was more natural than that the Christians celebrate the birth of Him Who was the 'Light of the World' and the true 'Sun of righteousness' on this very day? The popes seem to have chosen December 25 precisely for the purpose of inspiring the people to turn from the worship of a material sun to the adoration of Christ the Lord. This thought is indicated in various writings of contemporary authors.

"It has sometimes been said that the Nativity is only a 'Christianized pagan festival.' However, the Christians of those early centuries were keenly aware of the difference between the two festivals—one pagan and one Christian—on the same day. The coincidence in the date, even if intended, does not make the two [p. 62] celebrations identical. Some newly converted Christians who thoughtlessly retained external symbols of the sun worship on Christmas Day were immediately and sternly reproved."— Francis X. Weiser, *Handbook of Christian Feasts and Customs* (New York: Harcourt, Brace and World, Inc., 1958), 60-62.

IT WAS THE BIRTHDAY OF THE SUN GOD—"One of the dominant religious ideas of the second and third centuries was the belief in the divinity of the Sun . .

"This divinity is of especial interest for our inquiry, for his annual festival fell on the twenty-fifth of December and its relation to Christmas [p. 151] has been a matter of protracted discussion. Obviously the season of the winter solstice, when the strength of the sun begins to increase, is appropriate for the celebration of the festival of a sun-god. The day in a sense marks the birth of a new sun. But the reason for its being chosen as the day for the commemoration of Christ's nativity is not so evident.

" . . The identity of date is more than a coincidence. To be sure the Church did not merely appropriate the festival of the popular sun-god. It was through a parallelism between Christ and the sun that the twenty-fifth of December came to be the date of the nativity . . [p. 153] Even Epiphanius, the fourth century metropolitan of Cyprus, though giving the sixth of January as the date of birth, connects the event with the solstice. Moreover, the diversion of the significance of a popular pagan holiday was wholly in accord with the policy of the Church. Of the actual celebration of a festival of the nativity, it should be added, there is no satisfactory evidence earlier than the fourth century. Its first observance in Rome on December the twenty-fifth took place in 353 or 354 (Usener) or in 336 (Duchesne). In Constantinople it seems to have been introduced in 377 or 378."—Gordon J. Laing, *Survivals of Roman Religion* (New York: Longmans, 1931), 150-153.

THE PAGAN WORSHIPERS OF MITHRA CELEBRATED THE BIRTHDAY OF THE SUN ON DECEMBER 25—"Each day in the week, the planet to which the day was sacred was invoked in a fixed spot in the crypt; and Sunday, over which the Sun presided, was especially holy . .

"The rites which they [the Mithraists] practised offered numerous analogies . . They also held Sunday sacred, and celebrated the birth of the Sun [god] on the 25th of December."—Franz Cumont, *the Mysteries of Mithra*, Trans. by T.J. McCormack, 167, 191.

WORSHIPERS OF MITHRAS, THE SUN GOD, WON BY MAKING DECEMBER 25 THE BIRTHDAY OF CHRIST—"While Christianity won a comparatively easy victory over the Graeco-Roman religion, it had a hard struggle with the Mithras religion. The worshipers of Mithras were won by taking over the birthday of Mithras, December 25, as the birthday of Christ."—H. Larner, "Mithras," *Worterbuch der Antike*, 2nd ed.; Leipzig: A.

Kroner, 1933.

TWO MITHRAIC HOLY DAYS ADOPTED AS CHRISTIAN HOLY DAYS—"*Remains of the struggle are found in two institutions adopted from its rival by Christianity in the fourth century, the two Mithraic sacred days, December twenty-fifth, dies natalis solis [birthday of the sun], as the birthday of Jesus, and Sunday "the venerable day of the Sun," as Constantine called it in his edict of 321."—Walter Woodburn Hyde, Paganism to Christianity in the Roman Empire, 60.*

CHRISTMAS FALLS ON THE SUN'S BIRTHDAY, WHICH IS JUST AFTER DECEMBER 21, THE WINTER SOLSTICE—"*A very general observance required that on the 25th of December the birth of the 'new Sun' should be celebrated, when after the winter solstice the days began to lengthen and the 'invincible' star triumphed again over darkness. It is certain that the date of this Natalis Invicti was selected by the Church as the commemoration of the Nativity of Jesus, which was previously confused with the Epiphany. In appointing this day, universally marked by pious rejoicings, which were as far as possible retained,—for instance the old chariot races were preserved,—the ecclesiastical authorities purified in some degree the customs which they could not abolish. This substitution, which took place at Rome probably between 354 and 360, was adopted throughout the Empire, and that is why we still celebrate Christmas on the 25th of December.*

"*The pre-eminence assigned to the dies Solis also certainly [p. 90] contributed to the general recognition of Sunday as a holiday. This is connected with a more important fact, namely, the adoption of the week by all European nations."—Franz Cumont, Astrology and Religion Among the Greeks and Romans (reprint; New*

York: *Dover Publications, Inc., 1960), 89-90.*

SUMMARY OF PAGAN ORIGIN OF CHRISTMAS—
"It is admitted by the most learned and candid writers of all parties, that the day of our Lord's birth cannot be determined; and that, within the Christian church, no such festival as Christmas was ever heard of till the third century. Not till the fourth century was far advanced did it gain much observance. How, then, did the Romanish Church fix on December the 25th as Christmas Day? Why, thus? Long before the fourth century, and long before the Christian era itself, a festival was celebrated among the heathen at that precise time of the year, in honor of the birth of the son of the Babylonian queen of heaven; and it may fairly be presumed that, in order to conciliate the heathen and to swell the number of the nominal adherents of Christianity, the same festival was adopted by the Roman Church, giving it only the name of Christ.

"This tendency on the part of Christians to meet paganism halfway was very early developed; and we find Tertullian, even in his day, about the year 230, bitterly lamenting the inconsistency of the disciples of Christ in this respect, and contrasting it with the strict fidelity of the pagans to their own superstition . . Upright men strove to stem the tide, but in spite of all their efforts, the apostasy went on, till the church, with the exception of a small remnant, was submerged under pagan superstition.

"That Christmas was originally a pagan festival, is beyond all doubt. The time of the year, and the ceremonies with which it is still celebrated, prove its origin. In Egypt, the son of Isis, the Egyptian title for the queen of heaven, was born at this very time, 'about the time of the winter solstice.' The very name by which Christmas is popularly known among ourselves—Yule day—proves at

once its pagan and Babylonian origin. 'Yule' is the Chaldee name for an 'infant' or 'little child'; and, as the 25th day of December was called by our pagan Anglo-Saxon ancestors, 'Yule day,' or the 'Child's day,' and the night that preceded it, 'Mother night,' long before they came in contact with Christianity, that sufficiently proves its real character. Far and wide, in the realms of paganism, was this birthday observed.

"This festival has been commonly believed to have had only an astronomical character, referring simply to the completion of the sun's yearly course and the commencement of a new cycle. But there is indubitable evidence that the festival in question had a much higher reference than this—that it commemorated not merely the figurative birthday of the sun in renewal of its course, but the birthday of the grand Deliverer.

"Among the Sabeans of Arabia, who regarded the moon, and not the sun, as the visible symbol of the favorite object of their idolatry, the same period was observed as the birth festival. Thus we read in Stanley's 'Sabean Philosophy': 'On the 24th of the tenth month,' that is December, according to our reckoning, 'the Arabians celebrated the birthday of the Lord—that is, the moon.' The Lord Moon was the great object of Arabian worship, and that Lord Moon, according to them, was born on the 24th of December, which clearly shows that the birth which they celebrated had no necessary connection with the course of the sun.

"It is worthy of special note, too, that if Christmas day among the ancient Saxons of this land was observed to celebrate the birth of any lord of the host of heaven, the case must have been precisely the same here as it was in Arabia. The Saxons, as is well-known, regarded the sun as a female divinity, and the moon as a male. It must have been the birthday of the Lord Moon, there-

fore, and not of the sun, that was celebrated by them on the 25th of December, even as the birthday of the same Lord Moon was observed by the Arabians on the 24th of December."—*The Two Babylons, Alexander Hislop, 7th edition, 92-94.*

PAGAN PARALLELS TO THE SUN GOD BIRTH DATE—*"Babylonian influence becomes particularly prominent in the great Nabataean kingdom whose principal capitals were Petra [p. 16] and Damascus, and whose history can be traced from their first mention by Ashurbanipal in the middle of the seventh century B.C., to their absorption into the Roman Empire in A. D. 106. They were a North Arabic race who used the Aramaic script, and their principal male deity is Dusura, rendered into Greek as Doundares, and identified by the Greeks with Dionysus. The name means 'he of Shara' (dhu Sara), i.e., 'he of the mountain range esh-shara,' at Petra, and he is a Sun-god according to Strabo. Epiphanius, bishop of Salamis in Cyprus, writing in the fourth century, preserves the only illuminating information about the mythology of this great cult of the Nabataeans. As he was born and educated in Palestine, and served in a monastic order there, his statement must be taken authoritatively. He says that the Nabataeans praised the virgin whose Arabic name is Chaabou. In Nabataean the Arabic nominative ending in u is regularly preserved in proper names, and Epiphanius undoubtedly heard the word ka'bu, 'square stone,' symbol in Nabataean religion for both Dusares and the great Mother-goddess, Allat of the Nabataeans. An Arabic writer says that a four-sided stone was worshipped as Allat, who in a Nabataean inscription was called 'Mother of the gods' . . Epiphanius states that Dusares was the offspring of the virgin Chaabou and only son of the 'lord' (Ka'bu). The Panegyrarchs of Nabataean cities came to*

Petra to assist in the festival of his birth, which was celebrated on the twenty-fifth of December.

"Worship of a dying god, son of the Earth-mother, was the principal cult of this North Arabian people during the period immediately before and after the life of Jesus of Nazareth in Palestine. The title of the Mother-goddess, Allat, is 'Mother of the gods' here, and a translation of the title of the great Mother-goddess of Babylonia, *belet ilani*, 'queen of the gods,' whose title in Sumerian is also 'goddess Mother.' Dusares and Allat of the Nabataeans are an Arabian reflex of the great Babylonian myth of Tammuz and Ishtar; and if the god is identified with Dionysus, the original character common to both is that of a Sun-god and patron of fertility. Strabo describes the Nabataeans as a particularly abstemious people; the Greeks and Romans called Dusares the Arabian Dionysus or Bacchus; and a statue of him found in the Hauran portrays him as a deity of the vine. The cornucopia and patera are also characteristic of Dusares on coins of Nabataean cities as an Arabian. Bacchus Dusares is a Greek and Roman deity. The celebration of his birth in December at Petra and the northern cities of Bostra and Adraa in the Hauran with games and festivities is a replica of the spring festivities at Babylon, when the death, burial, and resurrection of Marduk were celebrated with weeping, which was exchanged for rejoicing. The meaning of the *actia dusaria* at Petra may be inferred from the similar festival at Alexandria in Egypt, there called after an unexplained Egyptian word Kikellia, or in Greek the Cronia, which also occurred by night on the twenty-fifth of December. In this festival an image of a babe was taken from the temple sanctuary and greeted with loud acclamation by the worshippers, saying, 'the Virgin has begotten.' On the night of the fifth of December, a festival occurred before the *image of Core; it ended with bringing forth from beneath the earth the image of Aion, which was carried seven times around the inner sanctuary of Core's temple. The image was then returned to its place below the surface of the earth. Epiphanius, in whose writing this Egyptian cult is described, identifies the virgin mother of this myth with the Greek underworld goddess Core, as he does the virgin mother of Dusares, Chaabou of the Nabataeans. There is a wide syncretism here in this Arabic religion, composed of Babylonian, Greek, and Egyptian elements; and beyond all doubt the Nabataeans possessed an elaborate cult of Tammuz and Ishtar, of Osiris and Isis, of Dionysus and Basilinna, the equivalent of Proserpine-Core, in which this deity was represented as a youth, son of the Mother-goddess, who was reborn yearly in midwinter and who died in the summer.*

"'The Mother-goddess of the Nabataeans, Allat, identified with Core by the Greeks, is essentially the North Semitic Astarte, and the Babylonian Ishtar.'"—Stephen H. Langdon, "Semitic Mythology," in Vol. 5 of The Mythology of All Races. Boston: Archaeological Institute of America, Marshall Jones Company, 1931, 15-19.

HEATHEN ORIGIN OF CHRISTMAS—*"The celebration of Christmas was not introduced in the church till after the middle of the fourth century. It originated in Rome, and was probably a Christian transformation of regeneration of a series of kindred heathen festivals, the Saturnalia, Sigillaria, Juvenalia, and Brumalia, which were celebrated in the month of December in commemoration of the golden age of universal freedom and equality, and in honor of the unconquered sun, and which were great holidays, especially for slaves and children. (See my [J.P. Lange's] Church History, N.Y., Vol. ii, 395 ff.) In the primitive church there was no agreement as to the time of Christ's birth. In the East the 6th of January* *was observed as the day of his baptism and birth. In the third century, as Clement of Alexandria relates, some regarded the 20th of May, others the 20th of April, as the birthday of our Saviour. Among modern chronologists and biographers of Jesus there are still greater differences of opinion; and every month, even June and July (when the fields are parched from want of rain), has been named as the time when the great event took place. Lightfoot assigns the nativity to September; Lardner and Newcome to October; Wieseler to February; Paulus to March; Greswell and Alford to the 5th of April, just after the spring rains, when there is an abundance of pasture. Luchtenstein places it in July or December, Strong in August; Robinson in autumn, Clinton in spring; Andrews between the middle of December, 749, to the middle of January, A.D. 750. On the other hand, Roman Catholic historians and biographers of Jesus, as Sepp, Friedlieb, Bucher, Patritius, also some Protestant writers, defend the popular tradition, of the 25th of December."—John Peter Lange, D.D., A Commentary on the Holy Scriptures, "Luke 2:36." New York: Charles Scribner & Co., 1870.*

CHRISTMAS WAS ORIGINALLY THE ROMAN FEAST OF SATURNALIA—*"The festival of Saturn fell on December 17, but its popular celebration lasted for seven days. It began as a country festival in the time when agriculture was one of the chief activities of the Romans. But soon it produced licentiousness and gambling. During these seven days city officials condoned conduct that they would not have tolerated at any other season. One feature of the occasion was the license allowed to slaves, who were permitted to treat their masters as if they were their social equals. Frequently indeed masters and slaves changed places and the latter were waited on by the former. Another feature of the cel-*

ebration was the exchange of gifts, such as candles (*cerei*) which are supposed to have symbolized the increasing power of the sunlight after the winter solstice, and little puppets of paste or earthenware (*sigillaria*), the exact significance of which is obscure. It was a season of hilarity and goodwill..

"The extremists who have said that Christmas was intended to replace the Saturnalia have vastly overstated the case. Nor is it of any importance that Epiphanius, the bishop of Salamis in Cyprus in the fourth century, places the Saturnalia on the twenty-fifth of December. This is not the only error in the list of dates in which it occurs. Without doubt, however, many of the customs of the Saturnalia were transferred to Christmas. Although the dates did not exactly coincide, for the Saturnalia proper fell on the seventeenth of December, the time of year was practically the same, and it has already been pointed out how frequently festivals of the merrymaking type occur among various peoples at this season. Fowler, mentioning the goodwill that so generally characterizes these celebrations, raises the question whether this was one of the reasons why Christmas was put at the winter solstice. Possibly, as has also been suggested, the postponement of the festivities from the date of the Saturnalia to Christmas week was in part at least caused by the institution of the Advent fast covering the period of the four Sundays before Christmas.

"Certainly many of the customs of the Christmas season go back to the Roman festival. In it lies the origin of the excessive eating and drinking, the plethora of sweets, the playing of games, and the exchange of gifts. Nor can we fail to connect our custom of burning candles with the candles (*cerei*) that were so conspicuously a part of the Saturnalia. Moreover, our Christmas holidays, like the Roman festival, are approximately a week

"In mediaeval times there were still other survivals, and the king of the Saturnalia is obviously the prototype not only of the Abbot of Unreason who at one time presided over the Christmas revels in Scotland, but also of the Lord of Misrule in England and the Abbe de Liesse in Lille. This mock dignitary had other titles . .

"We hear also of the Boy-Bishop (*Episcopus Puerorum*), whose authority lasted from St. Nicholas' day (December 6) till Childermas (December 28) and whose tradition (as well as that of the Bishop of Unreason) still survives to a certain extent on Santa Claus. Apparently the compromise bade by the Church in adapting the customs of the Saturnalia to Christian practice had little or no effect on checking the license of the festival. This continued through the whole Christmas festival and sometimes lasted till the day of Epiphany (January 6). We find many criticisms by churchmen or councils. In England Henry VIII issued a proclamation in 1542, abolishing the revels, but Mary restored them in 1554."—*Gordon J. Laing, Survivals of Roman Religion (New York: Longmans, 1931), 58, 62-65.*

CHRISTMAS DOWN THROUGH THE CENTURIES—"The great church adopted Christmas much later than Epiphany; and before the fifth century there was no general consensus of opinion as to when it should come on the calendar, whether on the 6th of January, of the 25th of March, or the 25th of December.

"The earliest identification of the 25th of December with the birthday of Christ is in a passage, otherwise unknown and probably spurious, of Theophilus of Antioch (A.D. 171-183), preserved in Latin by the Magdeburg Centuriators (i. 3, 118), to the effect that the Gauls contended that as they celebrated the birth of the Lord on the 25th of December, whatever day of the week it might be, so they ought to celebrate the Pascha on the 25th of March when the resurrection befell.

"The next mention of the 25th of December is in Hippolytus' (c. 202) commentary on *Daniel* 4:23. Jesus, he says, was born at Bethlehem on the 25th of December, a Wednesday, in the forty-second year of Augustus. This passage also is almost certainly interpolated. In any case he mentions no feast, nor was such a feast congruous with the orthodox ideas of that age. As late as 245, Origen, in his eighth homily on Leviticus, repudiates as sinful the very idea of keeping the birthday of Christ 'as if he were a king Pharaoh.' The first certain mention of December 25 is in a Latin chronographer of A.D. 354, first published entire by Mommsen. It runs thus in English: 'Year 1 after Christ, in the consulate of Caesar and Paulus, the Lord Jesus Christ was born on the 25th of December, a Friday and 15th day of the new moon.' Here again no festival celebration of the day is attested.

"There were, however, many speculations in the second century about the date of Christ's birth. Clement of Alexandria, toward its close, mentions several such, and condemns them as superstitions. Some chronologists, he says, alleged the birth to have occurred in the twenty-eighth year of Augustus, on the 25th of Pachon, the Egyptian month, i.e., the 20th of May. These were probably the Basilidian Gnostics. Others set it on the 24th or 25th of Pharmuthi, i.e., the 19th or 20th of April. Clement himself sets it on the 17th of November, 3 B.C. The author of a Latin tract, called the *De Pascha computus*, written in Africa in 243, sets it by private revelation, *ab ispo deo inspirsti*, on the 28th of March. He argues that the world was created perfect, flowers in bloom, and trees in leaf, therefore in spring; also at the equinox, and when the moon just created was full. Now the moon *and sun were created on a Wednesday. The 28th of March suits all these considerations. Christ, therefore, being the Sun of Righteousness, was born on the 28th of March. The same symbolic reasoning led Polycarp (before 160) to set his birth on Sunday, when the world's creation began, but his baptism on Wednesday, for it was the analogue of the sun's creation. On such grounds certain Latins as early as 354 may have transferred the human birthday from the 6th of January to the 25th of December, which was then a Mithraic feast and is by the chronographer above referred to, but in another part of his compilation, termed Natalis invicti solis, or birthday of the unconquered Sun. Cyprian (de orat. dom. 35) calls Christ Sol verous. Ambrose calls Him Sol novus noster (Sermo vii. 13), and such rhetoric was widespread. The Syrians and Armenians, who clung to the 6th of January, accused the Romans of sun worship and idolatry, contending with great probability that the feast of the 25th of December had been invented by disciples of Cerinthus and its lections by Artemon to commemorate the natural birth of Jesus ..*

"In Britain the 25th of December was a festival long before the conversion to Christianity, for Bede (De temp. rat., ch. 13) relates that 'the ancient peoples of the Angli began the year on the 25th of December when we now celebrate the birthday of the Lord; and the very night which is now so holy to us, they called in their tongue modranecht (modra niht), that is, the mothers' night, by reason we suspect of the ceremonies which in that night-long vigil they performed.' With his usual reticence about pagan or orthodox matters, Bede abstains from recording who the mothers were and what the ceremonies. In 1644 the English Puritans forbade any merriment or religious services by act of Parliament, on the ground that it was a heathen festival, and ordered it to

be kept as a fast. Charles II revived the feast, but the Scots adhered to the Puritan view."—*The Encyclopedia Britannica, Vol. VI, "Christmas," 293, 294, 11th edition.*

CHRISTMAS IN THE MIDDLE AGES AND BEYOND—"MIDDLE AGES. *The great religious pioneers and missionaries who brought Christianity to the pagan tribes of Europe also introduced the celebration of Christmas..*

"The period from the twelfth to the sixteenth centuries was the peak of a general Christian celebration of the Nativity.. It was at this period, too, that most of the delightful Christmas customs of each country were introduced. Some have since died out; others have changed slightly through the ages. Many have survived to our day. A few practices had to be suppressed as being improper and scandalous, such as the customs of dancing and mumming in church, the 'Boy Bishop's Feast,' the 'Feast of the Donkey,' New Year's fires, superstitious (pagan) meals, impersonations of the Devil, and irreverent carols.

"DECLINE. With the Reformation in the sixteenth century there naturally came a sharp change in the Christmas celebration for countries in Europe. The Sacrifice of the Mass—the very soul of the feast—was suppressed. The Holy Eucharist, the liturgy of the Divine Office, the sacramentals and ceremonies all disappeared. So did the colorful and inspiring processions, the generation of the Blessed Virgin Mary and the saints. In many countries all that remained of the once rich and glorious religious festival was a sermon and a prayer service on Christmas Day. Although the people kept many of their customs alive, the deep religious inspiration was missing, and consequently the 'new' Christmas turned more and more into a feast of good-natured reveling.

"On the other hand, some groups, including the German Lutherans, preserved a tender devotion to the Christ Child and celebrated Christmas in a deeply spiritual way within their churches, hearts, and homes.

"In England the Puritans condemned ever the reduced religious celebration that was held in the Anglican Church after the separation from Rome ..

"When the Puritans finally came to political power in England, they immediately proceeded to outlaw Christmas ..

"Revival in England. When the old Christmas eventually returned with the restoration of the monarchy in 1660, it was actually a 'new' Christmas. The spiritual aspect of the feast was left mostly to the care of the ministers in the church service on Christmas Day. What was observed in the home consisted of a more shallow celebration in the form of various nonreligious amusements and of general reveling .. However, a spirit of good will to all and of generosity to the poor ennobled these more worldly celebrations of the great religious feast. Two famous descriptions of this kind of popular celebration are found in Charles Dickins' *A Christmas Carol* and in Washington Irving's *Sketch Book* ..

"Christmas in America .. The feast was celebrated with all the splendor of liturgical solemnity and with the traditional customs of the respective nationalities in Florida, on the shores of the Gulf of Mexico, in Canada, and in the territory of the present State of Michigan.

"In the colonies of New England, however, the unfortunate and misdirected zeal of the Puritans against Christmas persisted far into the nineteenth century ..

"It was not until immigrants from Ireland and from continental Europe arrived in large numbers toward the middle of the last century that Christmas in America began to flourish. The Germans brought the Christmas tree. They were soon joined by the Irish, who contributed the ancient Gaelic custom of lights in the windows . .

"Very soon their neighbors shared in these unusual but attractive innovations, followed their example and made many of these customs their own."—*Francis X. Weiser, Handbook of Christian Feasts and Customs (New York: Harcourt, Brace and World, Inc., 1958), 62-67.*

SANTA CLAUS—St. Nicholas is thought to be a fine old saint in the church, but not so. It is true that there may have been a Nicholas, bishop of Myra, who lived in the fourth century and was said to have helped the poor. But Santa Claus was named after another "old Nick."

The legend of Santa Claus is quite similar to those of the ancient Egyptian god, Bes. Bes was a short rotund god who was said to give gifts to children. They were told he lived in the far north, where he spent most of the year making toys for them.

The Roman god, Saturn, was similar—and probably copied from Bes. He too was said to live in the northernmost part of the world, making gifts for children who were good. The Romans said he was the one who, each December, brought them the gifts of the new year.

The names, "Santa Claus" and "Kriss Kringle," do not go as far back into history. "Sant Nikolaas" (Sant-Ni-Klaus) and "Kriss Kringle" are from the German "Christ Krindl," or "Christ Child." So we have here a counterfeit Christ.

Parents punish their children for telling falsehoods, then tell them this big one in December! Later, when their children are grown, they wonder why they question the existence of God.

Teach your children about Jesus Christ—their best Friend, their only Saviour, and the only One who can really bring them the gifts they need. Do not waste time telling them myths; lest, when they grow older, they will not believe the realities you tell them of.

THE ORIGIN OF SANTA CLAUS—"When the Dutch came to America and established the colony of New Amsterdam, their children enjoyed the traditional 'visit of Saint Nicholas' on December 5; for the Dutch had kept this ancient Catholic custom even after the Reformation. Later, when England took over the colony and it became New York, the kindly figure of Sinter Klaas (pronounced Santa Claus) soon aroused among the English children the desire of having such a heavenly visitor come to their homes, too.

"The English settlers were glad and willing to comply with the anxious wish of their children. However, the figure of a Catholic saint and bishop was not acceptable in their eyes, especially since many of them were Presbyterians, to whom a bishop was repugnant. In addition, they did not celebrate the feasts of saints according to the ancient Catholic calendar.

"The dilemma was solved by transferring the visit of the mysterious man whom the Dutch called Santa Claus from December 5 to Christmas, and by introducing a radical change in the figure itself. It was not merely a 'disguise,' but the ancient saint was completely replaced by an entirely different character. Behind the name Santa Claus actually stands the figure of the pagan Germanic god Thor (after whom Thursday is named). Some details about Thor from ancient German mythology will show the origin of the modern Santa Claus tale:

"Thor was the god of the peasants and the common people. He was represented as an elderly man, jovial and friendly, of heavy build, with a long white beard. His element was the fire, his color red. The rumble and roar of thunder were said to be caused by the rolling of his *chariot, for he alone among the gods never rode on horseback but drove in a chariot drawn by two white goats (called Cracker and Gnasher). He was fighting the giants of ice and snow, and thus became the Yule-god. He was said to live in the 'Northland' where he had his palace among icebergs. By our pagan forefathers he was considered as the cheerful and friendly god, never harming the humans but rather helping and protecting them. The fireplace in every home was especially sacred to him, and he was said to come down through the chimney into his element, the fire.[70] [Note 70: H.A. Grueber, Myths of Northern Lands, Vol. I, New York, 1895, 61.] Here, then, is the true origin of our "Santa Claus." It certainly was a stroke of genius that produced such a charming and attractive figure for pagan mythology. With the Christian saint whose name he still bears, however, this Santa Claus has really nothing to do."—Francis X. Weiser, Handbook of Christian Feasts and Customs (New York: Harcourt, Brace and World, Inc., 1958), 113-114.*

MISTLETOE—*Where did the mistletoe custom originate? Among the ancients, because mistletoe was considered sacred to the sun, it was used at the December festival of the winter solstice, when the sun was lowest in the noon sky.*

Kissing under the mistletoe was thought to be an act of solar worship, empowering the worshipers for still further worship. As this indicates, pagan sun-worship services were very licentious. Temple prostitution was performed during the eight-day Roman Saturnalia which immediately preceded the December 25 sun-birth celebration.

MISTLETOE WAS THE SACRED PLANT OF THE HEATHEN DRUIDS—*"The mistletoe was a sacred plant in the pagan religion of the Druids in Britain. It was* believed to have all sorts of miraculous qualities: the power of healing diseases, making poisons harmless, giving fertility to humans and animals, protecting from witchcraft, banning evil spirits, bringing good luck and great blessings. In fact, it was considered so sacred that even enemies who happened to meet beneath a mistletoe in the forest would lay down their arms, exchange a friendly greeting, and keep a truce until the following day. From this old custom grew [p. 104] the practice of suspending mistletoe over a doorway or in a room as a token of good will and peace to all comers..

"After Britain was converted from paganism to Christianity, the bishops did not allow the mistletoe to be used in churches because it had been the main symbol of a pagan religion. Even to this day mistletoe is rarely used as a decoration for altars. There was, however, one exception. At the Cathedral of York at one period before the Reformation a large bundle of mistletoe was brought into the sanctuary each year at Christmas and solemnly placed on the altar by a priest. In this rite the plant that the Druids had called 'All-heal' was used as a symbol of Christ, the Divine Healer of nations.

"The people of England then adopted the mistletoe as a decoration for their homes at Christmas. Its old, pagan religious meaning was soon forgotten, but some of the other meanings and customs have survived: the kiss under the mistletoe; the token of good will and friendship; the omen of happiness and good luck and the new religious significance."—*Francis X. Weiser, Handbook of Christian Feasts and Customs (New York: Harcourt, Brace and World, Inc., 1958), 103-104.*

WREATHS AND HOLLY—"Circular wreaths of evergreen branches (especially holly) were a featured part of the festival. These were formed in the shape of the sun, and represented life which could not exist without sunlight. These wreaths were placed on inside and outside walls during the celebrations. At the time of initiation into the Dionysian mysteries, these were worn by the initiates as fertility symbols. They represented the perpetuity of existence through on-going cycles of life, death, and rebirth.

"Holly berries were also considered sacred to the sungod.

"The use of Christmas wreaths is believed by authorities to be traceable to the pagan customs of decorating buildings and places of worship at the feast which took place at the same time as Christmas."—*Frederick J. Haskins, Answers to Questions.*

CHRISTMAS TREES—Green trees were cut down, mounted, and then decked with offerings of food and precious gifts to Mithra.

"The Christmas tree is from Egypt, and it originally dates from a period long anterior to the Christian Era."—*Frederick J. Haskins, Answers to Questions.*

Evergreens, because of their ability to remain fresh and green throughout the year, symbolized immortality and fertility. Egyptian priests taught that the evergreen tree sprang from the grave of their god Osiris, who, after being murdered by another god, was resurrected through the energy in an evergreen tree.

Even the Bible speaks about the pagan custom:

"Thus saith the Lord, Learn not the way of the heathen . . For the customs of the people are vain: for one cutteth a tree out of the forest, the work of the hands of the workman, with the axe. They deck it with silver and with gold; they fasten it with nails and with hammers, that it move not."—*Jeremiah 10:2-4.*

YULE LOG—The Yule log did not come from the Bible, nor from Near Eastern paganism. It came from

Historians Tell Us More about Christmas

heathen Celtic worship practices in Britain. The Celts also worshiped the sun, and they too had a celebration at the time of the winter solstice. Their December sun festival, called *Julmond,* was taken into Christianity when it came to Britain. During the Yule festival, evergreen branches were used for decoration; and, after the branches were stripped off, the log was considered sacred to the sun. It was round like the sun and its length symbolized the movement, just as the sun was round and moved through the sky. (All this may sound ridiculous, but paganism always is.)

The family would, each year, go out and specially select a nice round tree from which to cut the yule log. When burned it sent out heat, just as the sun god burned and sent out heat.

CHRIST'S MASS—"Christmas" means "Christ's Mass." This is a special Roman Catholic mass performed on December 25. It must be attended by the faithful, under penalty of mortal sin for not doing so. At this mass—as at every other—Christ is offered by the priest in a wafer. The people are to worship this wafer as the true body, blood, mind, and soul of Jesus Christ!

One of the most recent Vatican statements on this reveals that this worship of a piece of bread remains unchanged:

"There should be no doubt in anyone's mind that all the faithful ought to show to this most holy sacrament [the communion wafer] the worship which is due to the true God, as has always been the custom of the Catholic Church. Nor is it to be adored any the less because it was instituted by Christ to be eaten."—*Vatican II: The Conciliar and Post Conciliar Documents.*

This Vatican II statement reaffirms the doctrinal statement made in 1648 at the Council of Trent (Session 13: *Decree on the Eucharist,* chap. 5, Denz. 878,

1648).

SHOULD WE THEN GIVE PRESENTS?—The pagan Romans exchanged food, small statues of gods, and trinkets to one another during the winter festival. The church, in adopting the custom, declared that this is to be done on December 25.

"The interchange of presents between friends is alike characteristic of Christmas and the Saturnalia, and must have been adopted by Christians from the pagans, as the admonition of Tertullian plainly shows."—*Bibiothica Sacra, Vol. 12, 153-155.*

Should we today give gifts to our friends and to those who need them? Yes, it is well to do this all through the year—especially to the needy. But our choicest gifts should be brought to Christ. For that we have a Biblical example:

"Now when Jesus was born in Bethlehem of Judaea . . And when they [the wise men] were come into the house, they . . fell down, and worshipped Him: and when they had opened their treasures they presented unto Him gifts; gold, and frankincense, and myrrh."—*Matthew 2:1, 11.*

Give Him the best you have; give Him your life. Dedicate all you have to Him, to be used in His service. Read the Bible daily and obey its commands through the enabling grace of Christ. Only then can you have genuine happiness.

But let not ancient paganism select the day on which you will worship God. The weekly Bible Sabbath was given as the day appointed us on which to worship Him. If we want to have happy gatherings with our loved ones, that is good. But let us not copy the heathen in doing it.

"Take heed to thyself that thou be not snared by following them . . That thou inquire not after their gods, saying, How did these nations serve their gods?

even so will I do likewise. Thou shalt not do so unto the Lord thy God: for every abomination to the Lord, which He hateth, have they done unto their gods."—Deuteronomy 12:30-31.

"In vain they do worship Me, teaching for doctrines the commandments of men."—Matthew 15:9.

It is obeying the Inspired Word of God—the Bible—the Sabbath He gave us (Genesis 2:1-3; Exodus 20, 8-11) and giving our lives in His service that we become worshipers of the Living God. That is what pleases Him, and we would rather please Him than do anything else. He has been so good to us all our lives. In Him we live and move and have our being, and only through Him can we be saved.

CHRISTMAS COUNTERFEITS OF CHRIST

SANTA vs. CHRIST

Comes in the night *vs.* Comes as a thief in the night (2 Peter 3:10, 1 Thess 5:2)

Dressed in white and red *vs.* Clothed in white and red (Rev 19:13-14, Isa 63:1-3)

Brings gifts and rewards *vs.* Brings gifts and rewards (Rom 6:23, Rev 22:12)

Knows if you've been good or not *vs.* Knows (Rev 2:23)

White, curly hair *vs.* White hair (Rev 1:14)

Sits and talks with children *vs.* Talks with children (Matt 19:14)

Comes with reindeer *vs.* Comes with horses (Rev 19:11, 14)

Comes with a sleigh *vs.* Comes with chariots (Isa 66:15)

Lives at the North Pole *vs.* Lives on the sides of the north (Ps 48:2)

Children tell him what they want *vs.* We pray to Him (Mat 7:7)

Santa Claus is not real, only imaginary *vs.* We should not take part in lies (Rev 22:14-15)

Old Saint Nick, one of Santa's names, is a name for Satan. (See "Old Nick" in the dictionary.)
The word, "Santa," unscrambled, is Satan.

Where Did Easter Come From?

Easter is a time for bunny rabbits, colored eggs, hot cross buns, and springtime apparel. Where did Easter come from? Here is the fascinating story of how it originated.

Few people realize that 'Easter' is not the resurrection of Christ; in fact, the only time the word is found in the Bible (in Acts 12:4), it is only 'Easter' by mistranslation. The word in the original Greek is 'Passover.'

Jesus died at the time of the Passover feast. But the Passover is not Easter, and Jesus did not die at Easter time. Here is information you will want to know. It comes from a publication entitled, "Easter: Where It Came From," printed many years ago, by Southern Publishing Association. An old man is speaking:

"The children had gathered around the huge, open fireplace. The lights were turned out and the shooting flames of the great wood fire lit their faces. Farther back, in a huge rocker, sat the Wise Man. In the daytime a very prosaic figure known as grandpa. On the special nights, when the children were allowed to 'stay up,' the fire light played on what seemed like the very soul of the old man, his face, and he became a mystic form, infinitely removed and yet very close to them. They called him the Wise Man then.

"This Easter night the children begged for the

Where Did Easter Come From?

story of Easter. They did not understand the first part of what he told, but afterward they understood nearly all of it.

"Here is what they learned:

"Sunday was held sacred centuries before Sinai. December 25 was highly honored; the time of Easter was religiously observed; and Lent was a time for healing—all thousands of years before the coming of the Babe to Bethlehem!"

"After the Flood, the Garden of Eden was no longer on the earth. You remember the Lord had placed angels with flaming swords at its gates. As the people came to the gates to worship God, their faces were toward the west, for the gates were on the east side of the Garden. When Eden was taken up to God's dwelling place, and no one knows just when that was, Satan had so confused some that they worshiped the things that God had made instead of God himself. The next brightest thing men saw was the sun, and they began to worship it. God at creation had given them the Sabbath, to remind them every week that He had made everything, but Satan has always tried to make men forget the Sabbath, so they would forget the true God.

"One of Noah's great grandsons was called Nimrod. Nimrod was a great leader, and was the first empire builder. His wife, history says, was named Semiramis, and she was a very great queen. Satan was working to counterfeit God's plan of salvation; and, when Nimrod died, the people said he was a god. Semiramis told them that he was indeed the sun god, and that his spirit was still living, dwelling, in the sun.

"In order that the people should love her as queen as long as she lived, Semiramis told them that hers was the spirit of the moon; and, when she died, she would dwell in the moon as Nimrod already dwelt in the sun.

46   *Christmas, Easter, and Halloween*

"Satan was laying the foundation for every system of falsehood and error the world has ever known. The sun god, under different names, was worshiped in Babylon, Egypt, Greece, and Rome, as conquering nations were conquered by the religion of their captives.

"Every year when the cold season began, the people believed their sun god was leaving them. They came to learn that his lowest dip on the horizon, about December 21, was followed by his gradual return, until in midsummer he was directly overhead at noonday. It was on the 25th of December that they noticed, each year, the coming back, a little, of their god. This day they called the birthday of the sun. It was this belief in the annual journey of their god that Elijah alluded to in his conflict with the priests of Baal, the Syro-Phoenician sun god *[1 Kings 18:19-40]*.

"After the death of Nimrod, Semiramis never married again—indeed how could the queen of heaven marry an ordinary man? But some years later she gave birth to a son. His name was Tammuz, and he was born on the 25th day of December! There was wild rejoicing in the nation over which Semiramis was queen. She told the people that the spirit of the sun, her husband Nimrod, was the father of Tammuz, and thus through her sin, Satan persuaded the people of the counterfeit birth of Jesus; for Jesus was really born of a virgin.

"Tammuz was hailed as the Son of the Sun, and the first letter of his name became in time the symbol of sun worship. Human sacrifices to the sun god were offered on this initial letter, made of wood, known as the cross. His birthday, December 25, was honored more and more, and the first day of the week was called the Sun's day, or Sunday. The people forgot God's Sabbath, and honored the day of the sun. To honor Semiramis they set aside a time in honor of the moon. This was the

Where Did Easter Come From?   47

first full moon after the vernal equinox, or the twenty-first of March. The first Sunday after this full moon was indeed a gala day.

"*While yet a young man, Tammuz, a hunter like his supposed father, was killed by a wild boar. What weeping there was in the kingdom! And the forty days before the time of the celebration for the moon were set apart as days of weeping for Tammuz.*

"*God's people were constantly being tempted to follow this religion instead of that of the Bible. Often Satan succeeded in his purpose. In the eighth chapter of Ezekiel we read of the women's weeping for Tammuz and the people's turning their backs on the temple of God and worshiping the sun toward the east. They also worshiped the moon goddess, making cakes to the queen of heaven (Jer. 7:18-19). These were round cakes on which had been cut a cross.*

"*The great distinguishing mark of the heathen was Sunday and the mark of God's people was the Sabbath (Eze. 20:12-20). Side by side through the centuries were God's people worshiping Him, obeying His commandments, keeping His Sabbath; and the heathen were worshiping the sun, keeping Sunday, offering their children in the fire as a sacrifice to the sun, or crucifying their human victims to turn away his supposed anger.*

"*One writer in a noted periodical says that 'Sunday was the wild, solar holiday of all pagan times.' It was on this day that the worst features of sun worship were practiced. Too often Israel did these things too, but God constantly sent them messages to obey Him.*

"*Finally Christ, the Son of God, was born. The exact day of His birth no one knows, but it was probably in October. He was just thirty-three and a half years old when He was crucified, in April, at the time of the Passover. How Jesus loved His people! He loved them so much* that He was willing to suffer abuse and mocking, scourging and death. Remember that Tammuz was exalted by Satan to be the great rival of Jesus, and the symbol of the cross was the sign of sun worship. Through all the years it had seemed that the sun god was greater than the true God, for Israel alone followed God, but often even Israel followed the sun god.

"Oh yes, Jesus loved His people! He came into a world that had forgotten Him, its Creator, suffered every insult at its hands, and finally died upon the symbol of sun worship, 'even,' says Paul, 'the death of the cross' (Phil. 2:8).

"What rejoicing then by the demons! The Son of God, delivered by His own people and crucified by the sun-worshiping Romans on the symbol of sun worship! Oh the condescending Jesus! How He must have loved His people!"

"The old man's face softened, and the children saw tears in his eyes. After a time he went on. His eyes were shining now.

"But God honored that sacrifice! On the third day after His crucifixion, the first day for sun worship, while the spirits of demons were in the wildest orgy of celebration over their victory; for, through many men, Satan's angels all rejoiced in the victory of false worship on that very day set aside and honored by the name of the sun—God raised His Son from the grave a conqueror! As after Creation He had rested, so after redemption He rested in the tomb on His Sabbath; and now, on the day of the sun, He was raised, eternal victor over the sun worship and all false systems of worship. That was why God raised Him on Sunday. Once more the Sabbath is God's sign between Him and His people. His disciples kept it while they lived.

Where Did Easter Come From?

"But Satan was not yet through with the world. First, he persecuted God's people, and then he tempted them again. The heathen were still keeping Sunday; and, as the Christians were scattered throughout the world, Satan whispered in the ears of God's people that they should try to gain favor by being more like the heathen. Was not Christ born toward the end of the year? The exact date was uncertain. Why not call it the same date as the birth of Tammuz? So December 25 became Christmas.

"Again, Christ was crucified and resurrected in the spring, near the time of the moon festival. Why not have the same time as the heathen, and even do as they did, but call it in honor of Christ's resurrection. The cakes to the queen of heaven became the hot cross buns. The forty days of 'weeping for Tammuz' became Lent; and at the close of Lent came Easter Sunday, a counterfeit masterpiece."

"The voice was silent for a time. The old man's face darkened as he seemed to see, in the embers of the fire, a sinister event against which he would cry out. Suddenly there rang out in the stillness the trumpet-like tones that had called to the men on the battlefield, when as a drummer boy, he had snatched up the colors where a dying bearer had fallen, and rallied a regiment that had nearly broken.

"Oh the cowards! The cowards! They allowed the flag of God, His holy Sabbath, to trail in the dust. They trampled it under their feet; they exalted the sun's day; they broke the command of God, and all in the name of the One who had given His life to save His people from that very thing!

"Oh, how Jesus in heaven must have wept when His so-called followers, to gain influence, set up the mark of rebellion against heaven—Sunday. And how He must *weep today when people profess to honor His resurrection by trampling on His day and honoring the flag of the defeated foe. God forgive our nation if she ever passes a law to do that, if she ever passes a national Sunday law."*

" 'Now all these things happened unto them for ensamples; and they are written for our admonition, upon whom the ends of the world are come. Wherefore let him that thinketh he standeth take heed lest he fall.' 1 Corinthians 10:11-12 . .

"It was by associating with idolaters and joining in their festivities that the Hebrews were led to transgress God's law and bring His judgments upon the nation. So now it is by leading the followers of Christ to associate with the ungodly and unite in their amusements that Satan is most successful in alluring them into sin. 'Come out from among them, and be ye separate, saith the Lord, and touch not the unclean.' 2 Corinthians 6:17.

"God requires of His people now as great a distinction from the world, in customs, habits, and principles, as He required of Israel anciently. If they faithfully follow the teachings of His Word, this distinction will exist; it cannot be otherwise. The warnings given to the Hebrews against assimilating with the heathen were not more direct or explicit than are those forbidding Christians to conform to the spirit and customs of the ungodly."

—*Patriarchs and Prophets, 457-458*

Additional Historical Facts about Easter

Easter began long before the time of Christ. Easter was the Ishtar celebration. Ishtar, Astarte, Ashtoreth were all the same. Under various names, a single pagan goddess was worshiped in different countries. As we trace the historical background of this goddess, we can see where Easter got its name, how our modern practice of sunrise worship originated, and why it is always commemorated at a certain time each spring. The story of Easter also helps explain how Sunday sacredness began and the origin of virgin worship.

In the following quotations, you will learn that, centuries before the birth of Christ, **Satan encouraged men in religious beliefs and practices which imitated the coming Saviour's resurrection, and prepared the world for the religious apostasy which would occur after the time of Christ.** *Here you will find a pagan god described, who was resurrected each spring on "Easter," a day which was dedicated to Ishtar, the mother goddess; she was also called the Queen of Heaven who interceded with the gods on behalf of mankind.*

This mother goddess was variously known as Astarte, Ishtar, Ashtoreth, Cybele, Demeter, Ceres, Aphrodite, Venus, and Freya.

"Astarte was the most important goddess of the pagan Semites. She was the goddess of love, fertility, and maternity for the Phonicians, Canaanites, Aramaeans, South Arabs, and even the Egyptians. Her name was Ishtar in Babylonia and Assyria, where she was also the goddess of war. Some Old Testament stories call her Ashtoreth, and describe the construction of her altar by King Solomon and its destruction by King Josiah. Astarte was identified with the planet Venus. The Greeks called her Aphrodite, and the Romans knew her as Venus."—World Book, Vol. 1, 782.

ASTARTE IN PHOENICA—Astarte was the goddess of the ancient Phoenicians. She loved Adoni (Adonis), who was slain by a boar (a wild pig), but rose from the dead and then ascended to heaven in the sight of his worshipers.

ASTARTE IN SYRIA—In Syria, Astarte was the Great Mother goddess and queen of prostitutes. Her worship culminated at the vernal equinox. This is about March 21 of each year, when the day and night are of equal length; we today call it the first day of spring. The well-known historian, Will Durant, explains how her lover was celebrated with sexual orgies, by the pagans, on March 21:

"Religious prostitution flourished, for in Syria, as throughout western Asia, the fertility of the soil was symbolized in a Great Mother, or goddess, whose sexual commerce with her lover gave the hint to all the reproductive processes and energies of nature; and the sacrifice of virginity at the temples was not only an offering to Astarte, but a participation with her in that annual self-abandonment which, it was hoped, would offer an irresistible suggestion to the earth, and insure the increase of plants, animals, and men.

"About the time of the vernal equinox, the festival of the Syrian Astarte, like that of Cybele in Phrygia, was celebrated at Hierapolis with a fervor bordering upon madness. The noise of flutes and drums mingled with the wailing of the women for Astarte's dead lord, Adoni; eunuch priests danced wildly, and slashed themselves with knives . . Then in the dark of the night, the priests brought a mystic illumination to the scene, opened the tomb of the young god, and announced triumphantly that Adoni, the lord, had risen from the dead. Touching the lips of the worshipers with balm, the priests whispered to them the promise that they, too, would some day rise from the grave."—Will Durant, History of Civilization, Vol. 1, 296-297.

ASHTORETH IN ISRAEL—The Israelites referred to Astarte as "Ashtoreth." In the Bible, the prophets of God denounced the worship of Ashtoreth, but many of the people worshiped her and her consort, Baal, the sun god. This worship was done amid groves of trees, on the summits of mountains. Here they worshiped sacred stones, practiced divination, and engaged in orgies as part of their worship of Ashtoreth and Baal. Because the myth of Astarte included the idea of a resurrected sun god, the sacred grove worship was carried on at daybreak as the sun was coming up.

The northern kingdom of Israel (Samaria) was destroyed because of such idolary. Later, King Josiah of Judah marched through it and tore down the altars to Baal, 'and them also that burned incense unto Baal, to the sun, and to the moon, and to the planets.' He 'defiled Topheth . . that no man might make his son or his daughter to pass through the fire to Molech'; and he smashed the altars that Solomon had built for Chemosh, Milcom, and Astarte (see 2 Kgs 23:2, 4, 10, 13).

ISHTAR IN SUMERIA AND BABYLONIA—Ishtar was the love goddess of the Babylonians. Her worship came down from earliest times in Sumeria, where her lover was Tammuz. She was the goddess of mothers and *prostitutes, and of love and war.*

"Though her worshipers repeatedly addressed her as 'The Virgin,' 'The Holy Virgin,' and The Virgin Mother,' this merely meant that her amours were free from all taint of wedlock."—Will Durant, History of Civilization, Vol. 1, 235.

Ishtar was said to be the daughter of Sin, the moon god. Her lover was Tammuz, the sun god. She was called the "Queen of Heaven" by her worshipers and their priests. According to the ancient myth, when Tammuz was slain by a wild animal, Ishtar raises him to life. Because of this, a yearly spring festival was held in honor of Ishtar, the mother goddess.

"[This is the] myth of Ishtar and Tammuz. In the Sumerian form of the tale, Tammuz is Ishtar's younger brother; in the Babylonian form, he is sometimes her lover, sometimes her son; both forms seem to have entered into the myths of Venus and Adonis, Demeter and Persephone, and a hundred scattered legends of death and resurrection . . To the Babylonians it was sacred history, faithfully believed and annually commemorated by mourning and wailing for the dead Tammuz, followed by riotous rejoicing over his resurrection."—Ibid., 238-239.

ISHTAR IN SUMERIA—*Even earlier in history, the Sumerians worshiped Innini, or Ishtar. Here is Durant's description of this mother goddess, who interceded for men with the gods.*

"[The city] Uruk worshiped especially the virgin earth goddess Innini, known to the Semites of Akkad as Ishtar—the loose and versatile Aphrodite-Demeter of the Near East. Kish and Lagash worshiped a Mater Dolorsa, the sorrowful mother-goddess, Ninkarsag, who, grieved with the unhappiness of men, interceded for them with the sterner deities."—Ibid., 127.

Additional Facts about Easter

CYBELE IN PHRYGIA—The myths surrounding Cybele were so much like those of Greece, that the Greeks called their goddess, Rhea Cybele, and considered the two divinities one. In Greece, her temple was at Athens. As usual, she resurrected her lover, Attis, each spring at the vernal equinox.

DEMETER IN GREECE—Throughout the Near East, this mother goddess was variously known as Astarte, Ishtar, Ashtoreth, Cybele, Demeter, Ceres, Aphrodite, Venus, and Freya.

She had a special lover (sometimes called her son; and, in one case, her daughter). Thus, for example, we have Isis and Horus, the sun god (Osiris was the son), in Egypt (in later Egypt, Osiris was called Serapis); Ishtar and Tammuz, in Babylon and Sumeria; Cybele and Attis, in Phrygia; Aphrodite and Adonis, in Syria; Atys and Bendis, in Asia; and Anaita and Haoma (later called Mithra), in Persia.

She also had a special son (who was sometimes the same as his father). So we have Isis and Osiris, in Egypt; Ishtar and Tammuz, in Babylonia; Astarte and Adonis, in Syria; Demeter and Persephone (and daughter), in Greece; and Cybele and Attis, in Phrygia.

In Greece, she is called Demeter; and she obtained the yearly resurrection, each spring, of her daugher (not a son in this instance), Persephone.

"Essentially it [the myth of Demeter and Persephone] was the same myth as that of Isis and Osiris, in Egypt; Tammuz and Ishtar, in Babylonia; Astarte and Adonis, in Syria; Cybele and Attis, in Phrygia. The cult of motherhood survived through classical times to take new life in the worship of Mary, the mother of God."—Will Durant, *History of Civilization*, Vol. 2, 178.

ARTEMIS IN IONIA—Ephesus was the major city

of Ionia; and its temple of Artemis (called Diana in Acts 19) was famous, for it was the largest Greek temple ever built.

CERES, IN POSEIDONIA—The temple of Ceres stood on the site of an earlier temple to Poseidon. Here Ceres was venerated.

VENUS OF THE ROMANS—Venus (also called Aphrodite) was equivalent to the earth fertility and love goddess of the other Near Eastern nations. According to some stories, her son was Aeneas, the ancestor of the Romans; according to others, Cupid. In Rome, every month was dedicated to a god, and April belonged to Venus. She was worshiped as the Mother goddess of their race, since they were supposed to be descended from her through Aeneas. Later, they dedicated their days to gods and borrowed, from the Persians, the sacred sun god, Mithra, on that day.

ANAITA AND MITHRA OF PERSIA—As we pass down through time, we come to Persia and the goddess Anaita—the love, or earth, goddess. **Their chief god was the sun god, Ahura-Mazda, who later became known as Mithra (also called Mithras). Under the name, Mithra, he became the most important god in Rome before Christianity won out.**

"For a while, under Darius II [521-486], it [the worship of Ahura-Mazda] became the spiritual expression of a nation at its height .. Underneath the official worship of Ahura-Mazda, the cult of Mithra and Anaita—god of the sun and goddess of vegetation and fertility, generation and sex—continued to find devotees; and in the days of Artaxeres II [404-359 B.C.] their names began to appear again in the royal inscriptions. Thereafter Mithra grew powerfully in favor and Ahura-Mazda faded away until, in the first centuries of our era, the

Additional Facts about Easter

cult of Mithra as a divine youth of beautiful countenance—with a radiant halo over his head as a symbol of his ancient identity with the sun—spread throughout the Roman Empire, and shared in giving Christmas to Christianity [footnote on the same page]. Christmas was originally a solar festival, celebrating, at the winter solstice, the lengthening of the day and the triumph of the sun over his enemies. It became a Mithraic, and finally a Christian, holy day."—Will Durant, *History of Civilization*, Vol. 1, 372.

The leading gods of ancient Persia were Mithra, the sun god; Anaita, the nature goddess; and her lover Haoma, who rose to life again. Later, the dying-rising Haoma became transformed into the dying-rising Mithra, the saviour god who, in the hands of Satan, became the chief counterfeit of Christianity in the Roman Empire after the time of Christ. Mithra worship was a carefully contrived counterfeit of Christianity, which Satan suggested to the minds of men over the centuries.

But then, in the fourth century A.D., when Christianity won over Mithraism, Mithraic and Ishtar elements of worship were incorporated into Christian worship also.

Mithra was always shown with a **solar halo around his head**; so portraits and statues of Christ, Mary, and the saints also had halos around their heads.

Because worshipers of Ishtar presented her with two fertility symbols—**eggs and bunny rabbits**—these became part of the Christian Easter service.

Because **sunrise on Sunday morning**, at the beginning of spring, was next to December 25th, the holiest day in the Mithraic calendar, the practice of Easter sunrise services continued on into Christianity.

Because Mithra was **worshiped on the first day of**

the week, which the Persians and Romans called the sun day, Sunday sacredness—which is nowhere to be found in the Bible—came into the Christian church.

Because **Mithra, the sun, "died and rose to life" each year on December 25** (when the sun became lowest in the sky), the birth of Christ began to be celebrated on that date (although it is clear from facts in the Bible that He was born in the fall of that year).

Because **the Istar (Astarte, Astoreth, etc.) celebration was held each spring on a Sunday, close to the vernal equinox, the ascension of Christ was changed from 40 days after the time of Passover (as told us in the Bible) to the annual Easter celebration.**

All this began centuries before in paganism, with the Ishtar and Tammuz legend.

We have carefully considered what ancient, secular historical records reveal. Here are facts from another ancient historical record, the Bible:

At the beginning of earth's history, God created the entire world in six days and rested on the seventh day and sanctified it, setting it apart as a special day for men to worship Him on *(Gen 2:1-3)*. This is God's own day to worship Him on.

Jesus Christ created all things *(Col 1:16, John 1:3, Heb 1:2)*; and He calls Himself the Lord of the Sabbath *(Matt 12:8, Mark 2:28)*. It is His day—the Lord's day *(Rev 1:10)*.

He made it for man—all mankind—*(Mark 2:27)*, not just for the Jewish race. God gave the Sabbath at the foundation of the world *(Gen 2:1-3)*; and His followers kept it before it was given on Mount Sinai *(Ex 16)*. On Mount Sinai He spoke and wrote His law, so that all the world might more clearly know it *(Ex 20:8-11)*. In the fourth commandment, we find the seal of the law and

Additional Facts about Easter

the sign that He is our Creator *(Ex 20:11)* and our Redeemer *(Eze 20:12)* and that we belong to Him *(Eze 20:20).*

Jerusalem was destroyed and His people were led into captivity because they were so proned to idolatry and refused to obey Him and keep His Sabbath *(Jer 26:1-6, 52:1-13).*

While here on earth, Jesus gave a careful example of obedience to the Sabbath day which He had given mankind *(Luke 4:16)* and rebuked man-made changes in His laws *(Matt 15:9, 6)*. He magnified the law and made it honorable *(Matt 5:17-18).*

Just before His death He predicted the destruction of Jerusalem thirty-nine years later, in A.D. 70, and at the end of the world *(Matt 24)*. He also cautioned His followers to continue to carefully observe the Sabbath even when those terrible events should come to pass years, and even centuries, later *(Matt 24:20).*

He carefully instructed His disciples to keep His day holy; and He wanted them to "remember the Sabbath day" *(Ex 20:8)* long after He had returned to Heaven. His followers faithfully kept it after His death *(Luke 23:56)* and later in their missionary work *(Acts 13:14-16, 40-46;16:12-15; 17:1-4)*. They declared that we ought to obey God rather than men *(Acts 5:29)*. And Paul could sincerely say of himself and his follow believers: "Do we then make void the law through faith? God forbid: yea we establish the law" *(Rom 3:31)*. The Word of God was being fulfilled in order that the Gentiles would one day faithfully keep the Sabbath that the Jews were desecrating *(Isa 56:3-7).*

The Bible predicted that a great desolating power was to arise in later centuries that would seek to destroy the atonement and God's laws from among His people *(Dan 7:8, 20-21, 25; 8:9-12).*

The attempt, by this power, to change God's laws, and especially His law regarding time, was specifically predicted in Daniel 7:25. Only God can change the law, and so Paul predicted the rise of a man who would call himself God (2 Thess 2:3-4). With boldness this power would sit in the temple of God and call itself God (2 Thess 2:4) and boastfully admit what it had done, declaring it to be a mark of its authority—and, indeed, is it not? You see, it's like this: I acknowledge and honor God's authority when I obey His commands and encourage others to do so. I declare my independence of God when I set aside His law and refuse to keep it. But I set myself up as a rival god when, having set aside His law, I establish in its place a counterfeit and then require others to keep it in place of the law that God commanded!

"Whom ye obey, his servants ye are" (Rom 6:16). God's Word declares that obedience to this man-made god, by keeping his counterfeit day of worship (while knowing that there is not one word or hint in all the Scriptures to keep that false day in place of the true Sabbath) will soon bring upon oneself the Mark of the Beast (Rev 13:16-17, 14:6-12). Only the remnant who keep the commandments of God and the faith of Jesus at that time resist it (Rev 13:8, 14:6-12, 12:17). In fact, the Bible predicts a return to the true Sabbath. God's people will rebuild the torn-out place in the law of God by again keeping His true Sabbath (Isa 58:13-14). And thank God, the assuring prophecy is given that the saved of all ages will one day soon honor the holy Sabbath of God throughout all eternity in the new earth (Isa 66:22-23).

Sunday is never called sacred or holy anywhere in the Bible. It is never called the Sabbath or the Lord's Day. Sunday is only mentioned eight times in the Bible. The first time is Genesis 1:5, where the first day of cre-

Additional Facts about Easter

ation week is spoken of. The next five times refer to Jesus' appearances, on Sunday, to His disciples after His rest in the tomb on the Sabbath (Matt 28:1; Mark 16:1-2, 9; Luke 24:1; John 20:1, 18-19). Jesus went and found them and told them the good news that He was alive. There is nothing here about Sunday sacredness. The seventh time is in Acts 20:7-8, where Paul speaks to the Ephesian leaders. A few verses later (Acts 20:15-38), he speaks to another group in the middle of the week, but that doesn't make that day anymore sacred than the Sunday preceding it. For only a direct command of God can make a day holy. Repeatedly in Acts, Paul kept the Sabbath holy (Acts 13:14-16, 40-46; 16:12-15; 17:1-4) just as his Master had done before Him. Acts is as silent on Sunday sanctity as is Matthew, Mark, Luke, and John.

The eighth and last text is found in *1 Corinthians 16:1-2*, where Paul instructs the believers to do their bookkeeping at home on Sunday mornings. The first working day of the week was a good day for this, since Friday they were so busy preparing for the Sabbath.

—But what about the "Lord's Day"? John the Revelator saw Christ in vision on the Lord's Day (Rev. 1:10). What day was that? The Bible does not say it was Sunday; but, from statements elsewhere in the Bible, we can know what day it was.

The "Lord's Day," both in Greek as well as English, means "the Day of the Lord." The Sabbath is the day unto the Lord (Ex 20:10, Lev 23:3, Deut 5:14), His own day (Isa 58:13). Jesus is the Creator who gave us the Sabbath" (Eph 3:9, John 1:3, Col 1:16, Heb 1-2, Gen 2:1-3). John heard Him call Himself, "the LORD of the Sabbath day" (Matt 12:8, Mark 2:28). John well-knew which day was the Lord's Day. This day is the memorial day of the Creator (Gen 2:1-3, Ex 31:17), the memorial day of the Redeemer (Eze 20:12, 20). It is the Lord's Day .. a day that God wants to share with you. He plans to keep it with you throughout all eternity to come (Isa 66:22-23). Come, worship Him on the best day—His day—the only day of worship your God ever gave you.

For much more information on how a variety of pagan customs came into the Christian church in the first three centuries, read our book, *Mark of the Beast*.

"Little by little, at first in stealth and silence and then more openly as it increased in strength and gained control of the minds of men, 'the mystery of iniquity' carried forward its deceptive and blasphemous work.

"Almost imperceptibly the customs of heathenism found their way into the Christian church. The spirit of compromise and conformity was restrained for a time by the fierce persecutions which the church endured under paganism.

"But as persecution ceased, and Christianity entered the courts and palaces of kings, she laid aside the humble simplicity of Christ and His apostles for the pomp and pride of pagan priests and rulers; and in place of the requirements of God, she substituted human theories and traditions.

"The nominal conversion of

Constantine, in the early part of the fourth century, caused great rejoicing; and the world, cloaked with a form of righteousness, walked into the church.

"Now the work of corruption rapidly progressed. Paganism, while appearing to be vanquished, became the conqueror . . and superstitions were incorporated into the faith and worship of the professed followers of Christ."

—*Great Controversy, 49-50*

"The religion which is current in our day is not of the pure and holy character that marked the Christian faith in the days of Christ and His apostles. It is only because of the spirit of compromise with sin, because the great truths of the word of God are so indifferently regarded, because there is so little vital godliness in the church, that Christianity is apparently so popular with the world."

—*Great Controversy, 48*

Where Did Halloween Come From?

With the loving approval of their parents, children dress up in weird costumes and play pranks on Halloween night, little realizing that, for over a thousand years, this has been the one evening in the year specially dedicated by spirit mediums and witches to the worship of Satan.

Halloween has nothing to do with Christianity. It is a festival which no one—child or adult—should have anything to do with. We need to better understand the origins of Halloween and its dangers.

Here is where Halloween came from:

During the Dark Ages, a number of pagan customs were adopted by the dominant Christian church in Europe. One of these was devil night, which was later named, "Halloween." This special night, celebrated, since antiquity, as the night when the devils come out and walk about the streets, was a satanic festival on October 31 of each year. The next day was called "All Saints' Day" (or Allhallows Day or All Souls Day), so "Halloween" was the name given to "hallows evening," or the "evening before hallows day"). Like the night before it, Allhallows Day was dedicated to honoring the dead.

The Druids were an order of priests in Gaul (ancient France) and Britain. They were devil worshipers who told the people they must hold an annual celebra-

Where Did Halloween Come From?

tion to their two leading gods: the Celtic sun god and their lord of the dead. On this night, the god who brings death—Satan—was worshiped in a variety of peculiar ways. This October 31 festival was named Samhain (or Sowein; both are pronounced "SAH-win") or "summer's end." The next day, the sun god was worshiped.

On the night of October 31, they believed the dead came out of the graves and walked around; so they offered up sacrifices and had special feasts to honor them. The priests of Druid taught them that if they did not do this, when they themselves died they would be reincarnated as animals instead of people.

But pretended communication with the dead is the basis of spiritualism (also called spiritism), which is one of the most dangerous practices in society; for it invites the control of demons! We should have nothing to do with anything connected with spiritism. And that includes participating in Halloween.

Druidic priests became nominally converted to Christianity when, in the early centuries, it entered their land (A.D. 433-475), and Druidic practices, including the October 31 festival to devils, came into the church (A.D 558) at that time. To pacify the followers of Druid, in the eighth century, Pope Gregory III (A.D. 731-741) declared November 1 to be a special feast day honoring the dead. In the ninth century, Pope Gregory IV (827-844) said that it must be kept by all Christians. Church discipline would be enforced on those who refused.

It is of interest that November 1 was the first day of the Druidic New Year. This made the evening before very special. As might be expected, because the night of October 31 had for centuries been dedicated to devils, the new church ruling only intensified the celebrations that took place that night. The devils made sure of that. Soon Halloween (Hallowe'en, Allhallows Eve), originally a pagan festival, became the outstanding Christian event held every autumn.

Celebrations of all kinds took place. In Ireland, carvings on pumpkins and jack-o'-lanterns (also known as will-o'-the-wisp, fox fire, fairie fire, friar's lantern, and corpse lantern) were made. The legend was that a man named Jack had played practical jokes on the devil and bothered him, so the devil kept him out of heaven. Jack, therefore, had to live forever on earth carrying about a lit lantern, warning people not to offend the devil. The lesson for little children: Do not offend the devil.

Yet such teachings did not help either the people nor the morals of society. Throughout Europe, on this one night of the year, it soon seemed as if all the devils came out! Indeed, that was the hidden meaning of Halloween, and the wild excitement and orgies of the people on that night seemed to fulfill it.

The Druids believed that, on Halloween, ghosts, spirits, fairies, witches, and elves emerged from the woods and flew in from the skies to harm people. Those evil creatures must be placated with offerings of food. On that night, the Celts went with their children to one another's house to gather food for the devil gods.

Animals were feared on that night also. Dogs, owls, snakes, and pigs were particularly worshiped on that night; but, among them, the cat was regarded with a special veneration. The Druid priests taught that cats—especially black ones—were sacred. This is why, today, we think of cats, as well as skeletons, pumpkins, skulls, and children with sheets over their heads (imitating ghosts), when we think of Halloween.

Druids were supposed to be able to cast spells and bring demon spirits into cats and similar animals. By believing those lies, the people feared the priests and were in bondage to do whatever they requested.

Where Did Halloween Come From?

The Celtic priests also taught that witches ride on brooms through the skies on that night and fling down curses on those who do not honor the dead by taking part in the ritual ceremonies of that night.

As might be expected, Satan had introduced a similar October festival on the mainland of Europe among the Finns and Goths. However, it was the Druidic festival in Britain—and the date of that festival—which was adopted by the Vatican as the official harvest festival in honor of the dead.

After being adopted by nominal Christianity in the Dark Ages, the festival of Halloween spread throughout Europe and to most countries which they later colonized. Yet few today are aware that this holiday originated in paganism, not Christianity, and that it is the most dangerous "holiday" in the year. For long ages, Halloween has been a night especially dedicated to satanic agencies. Every October 31 we see the clearest evidence of that fact.

The Druid priests in North Wales taught that the devils came out of the fire on this night. So bonfires were lit, to bring them out in droves! This is why outdoor night fires are today considered a part of the Halloween experience.

In North Wales, each family was told to build a bonfire and then throw stones into it, to bring out the devils and placate the dead. Prayers were offered. In the Scottish highlands, fortune telling was done by clairvoyants during the bonfire celebrations.

The problem has become so serious in our time, that, a couple years ago in Detroit, Mayor Coleman Young reported that 281 fires occurred on that night, up 20 percent from the 223 fires set on the previous Halloween.

Another ancient Halloween practice was prognostication. Events of the forthcoming year (which began the next day) were predicted. The spirits were thought to give this information to the priests on that special evening. By accepting these speculations as truth, the people came to fear the power of the priests even more. It is well-known, among spiritist mediums, that those people who follow horoscopes and go to fortune tellers are easier to control. If you want devils to harass your life, then go to the prognosticators, the fortune tellers.

Our only safety is in fleeing to Christ and pleading for His protection. If we do that, regardless of our past, we will be safe.

Even today, it is at the time of this October devil festival that the psychics (a modern name for spiritist mediums) write down and publish their predictions of the following year's events. (It is of interest that lists of these predictions made by mystics have been compiled—and then checked out the following year. Only rarely does even one predicted event occur.) Have nothing to do with fortune telling, astrology, and horoscopes. Remember where they came from and the demon power controlling them.

After the papal edicts were given, adopting and "sanctifying" the October 31 festival into the church, the people were taught that, the next day, special masses must be said for the dead. Children were sent out to the homes on the evening before. The people were told to either give money or some other offering that night or fast the next day, so that departed souls might be released sooner from the suffering of purgatory. Because it was simpler to do, most gave Halloween offerings. In this way, the Druidic practice of begging food from home to home continued. The church of the Dark Ages was expert at absorbing pagan customs and then calling them "Christian."

Where Did Halloween Come From?

There are those today who have tried to "Christianize" Halloween Eve even more. They dress their children in Biblical costumes and celebrate Halloween as a "harvest festival." But the origin of the night's celebrations remains the same. We should not ape the world in observing special sacred days originated by Satan. Separation is needed, not compromise.

Vandalism on a major scale now plagues cities on that night. Not long ago, one U.S. city experienced three days of riots, arson, and mass destruction. For three days children and men seemed possessed, and the city seemed out of control.

Should we today celebrate this pagan night, which every witch, clairvoyant, wizard, and spirit medium will tell you is the outstanding occultic night in the year? Far better to keep our children home on that night, pray to God, and read the Bible! Dedicate year life anew to the true God, and shun the amusements and follies of the devil gods. Although very inviting, they will only bring you trouble and misery, confusion of mind, and an empty life without happiness.

To conclude this chapter, here are two significant statements by historians:

"*Druidic element:* Unlike the familiar observance of All Souls, Halloween traditions have never been connected with Christian religious celebrations of any kind. Although the name is taken from a great Christian feast (Allhollows' Eve), it has nothing in common with the Feast of All Saints and is, instead, a tradition of pre-Christian times that has retained its original character in form and meaning.

"Holloween customs are traced back to the ancient Druids . . Halloween fires are kindled in many places even now, especially in Wales and Scotland.

"Another, and more important, tradition is the Druidic belief that during the night of November 1 demons, witches, and evil spirits roamed the earth in wild and furious gambols of joy to greet the arrival of 'their season'—the long nights and early dark of the winter months. They had their fun with the poor mortals that night, frightening, harming them, and playing all kinds of mean tricks.

"The only way, it seemed, for scared humans to escape the persecution of the demons was to offer them things they liked, especially dainty food and sweets. Or, in order to escape the fury of these horrible creatures, a human could disguise himself as one of them and join in their roaming. In this way they would take him for one of their own and he would not be bothered. That is what the people did in ancient times, and it is in this very form the custom has come down to us, practically unaltered, as our familiar Holloween celebration . .

"*Roman element:* In those countries that once belonged to the Roman Empire there is the custom of eating or giving away fruit, especially apples, on Holloween. It spread to neighboring countries: to Ireland and Scotland from Britain, and to the Slavic countries from Austria. It is probably based upon a celebration of the Roman goddess Pomona, to whom gardens and orchards were dedicated. Since the annual Feast of Pomona was held on November 1, the relics of that observance became part of our Holloween celebration, for instance the familiar tradition of 'ducking' for apples."—Francis X. Weiser, Handbook of Christian Feasts and Customs, 315-316.

"Our pagan forefathers kept several 'cult of the dead' rites at various times of the year. One of these periods was the great celebration at the end of the fall and the beginning of the winter (around November 1). Together with the practices of nature and demon lore (fires, mas-

Where Did Halloween Come From?

querades, fertility cults) they also observed the ritual of the dead with many traditional rites. Since All Saints and All Souls happened to be placed within the period of such an ancient festival, some of the pre-Christian traditions become part of our Christian feast and associated with Christian ideas.

"There is, for instance, the pre-Christian practice of putting food at the graves or in the homes at such times of the year when the spirits of the dead were believed to roam their familiar earthly places. The beginning of November was one of these times. By offering a meal or some token of food to the spirits, people hoped to please them and to avert any possible harm they could do. Hence came the custom of baking special breads in honor of the holy souls and bestowing them on the children of the poor. This custom is widespread in Europe. 'All Souls' bread' is made and distributed in Germany, Hungary, and in the Slavic countries.

"In some sections of central Europe boys receive on All Souls' Day a cake shaped in the form of a hare, and girls are given one in the shape of a hen (an interesting combination of 'spirit bread' and fertility symbols). These figure cakes are baked of the same dough as the festive cakes that people eat on All Saints' Day and which are a favorite dish all over central Europe. They are made of braided strains of sweet dough and called 'All Saints' cakes" (Heiligenstriezel in German, Strucel Swiateczne in Polish, Mindszenti Kalácska in Hangarian)."—Francis X. Weiser, Handbook of Christian Feasts and Customs, 312-313.

"Nearly all forms of ancient sorcery and witchcraft were founded upon a belief in communion with the dead . . This custom of consulting the dead is referred

to in the prophecy of Isaiah: 'When they shall say unto you, Seek unto them that have familiar spirits, and unto wizards that peep and that mutter: should not a people seek unto their God? for the living to the dead? Isaiah 8:19.

"The same belief in communion with the dead formed the cornerstone of heathen idolatry. The gods of the heathen were believed to be the deified spirits of departed heroes. Thus the religion of the heathen was a worship of the dead . .

"The deification of the dead has held a prominent place in nearly every system of heathenism, as has also the supposed communion with the dead. The gods were believed to communicate their will to men, and also, when consulted, to give them counsel. Of this character were the famous oracles of Greece and Rome.

"The belief in communion with the dead is still held, even in professedly Christian lands. Under the name of spiritualism the practice of communicating with beings claiming to be the spirits of the departed has become widespread. It is calculated to take hold of the sympathies of those who have laid their loved ones in the grave. Spiritual beings sometimes appear to persons in the form of their deceased friends, and relate incidents connected with their lives and perform acts which they performed while living. In

Where Did Halloween Come From?

this way they lead men to believe that their dead friends are angels, hovering over them and communicating with them. Those who thus assume to be the spirits of the departed are regarded with a certain idolatry, and with many their word has greater weight than the Word of God . .

"Modern spiritualism and the forms of ancient witchcraft and idol worship—all having communion with the dead as their vital principle—are founded upon that first lie by which Satan beguiled Eve in Eden: 'Ye shall not surely die: for God doth know that in the day ye eat thereof . . ye shall be as gods.' Genesis 3:4-5. Alike based upon falsehood and perpetuating the same, they are alike from the father of lies."

—*Patriarchs and Prophets, 684-685*

"In the name of Christ I would address His professed followers: Abide in the faith which you have received from the beginning. 'Shun profane and vain babblings.' 2 Timothy 2:16. Instead of putting your trust in witchcraft, have faith in the living God. Cursed is the path that leads to Endor or to Ekron. The feet will stumble and fall that venture upon this forbidden ground. There is a God in Israel, with whom is deliverance for all who are oppressed. Righteousness is the foundation of His throne."

—*Counsels on Health, 458*

Additional Facts about Halloween

In order to better understand the inner meaning of Halloween, we need to see it in light of what God thinks about such activities. It is urgent that we understand the Word of God on these matters.

Few people realize how very dangerous it is to dabble in spiritism. Here is a powerful warning, excerpted from portions of pages 533-562 of the book, Great Controversy. This will help you understand the seriousness of the matter:

"Immortality, promised to man on condition of obedience, had been forfeited by transgression. Adam could not transmit to his posterity that which he did not possess; and there could have been no hope for the fallen race had not God, by the sacrifice of His Son, brought immortality within their reach. While 'death passed upon all men, for that all have sinned,' Christ 'hath brought life and immortality to light through the gospel.' Romans 5:12, 2 Timothy 1:10. And only through Christ can immortality be obtained. Said Jesus: 'He that believeth on the Son hath everlasting life: and he that believeth not the Son shall not see life' (John 3:36). Every man may come into possession of this priceless blessing if he will comply with the conditions. All 'who by patient continuance in well-doing seek for glory and honor and immortality,' will receive 'eternal life.' Romans 2:7.

"The only one who promised Adam life in disobedi-

Additional Facts about Halloween

ence was the great deceiver. And the declaration of the serpent to Eve in Eden—'Ye shall not surely die'—was the first sermon ever preached upon the immortality of the soul. Yet this declaration, resting solely upon the authority of Satan, is echoed from the pulpits of Christendom and is received by the majority of mankind as readily as it was received by our first parents. The divine sentence, 'The soul that sinneth, it shall die' (Ezekiel 18:20), is made to mean: The soul that sinneth, it shall not die, but live eternally. We cannot but wonder at the strange infatuation which renders men so credulous concerning the words of Satan and so unbelieving in regard to the words of God . .

" 'The wages of sin is death; but the gift of God is eternal life through Jesus Christ our Lord.' Romans 6:23. While life is the inheritance of the righteous, death in the portion of the wicked. Moses declared to Israel: 'I have set before thee this day life and good, and death and evil.' Deuteronomy 30:15. The death referred to in these scriptures is not that pronounced upon Adam, for all mankind suffer the penalty of his transgression. It is 'the second death' that is placed in contrast with everlasting life.

"In consequence of Adam's sin, death passed upon the whole human race. All alike go down into the grave. And through the provisions of the plan of salvation, all are to be brought forth from their graves. 'There shall be a resurrection of the dead, both of the just and the unjust'; 'for as in Adam all die, even so in Christ shall all be made alive.' Acts 24:15; 1 Corinthians 15:22. But a distinction is made between the two classes that are brought forth. 'All that are in the graves shall hear His voice, and shall come forth; they that have done good, unto the resurrection of life; and they that have done evil, onto the resurrection of damnation.' John 5:28, 29.

They who have been 'accounted worthy' of the resurrection of life are 'blessed and holy.' 'On such the second death hath no power.' *Revelation 20:6.* But those who have not, through repentance and faith, secured pardon, must receive the penalty of transgression—'the wages of sin.' They suffer punishment varying in duration and intensity, 'according to their works,' but finally ending in the second death. Since it is impossible for God, consistently with His justice and mercy, to save the sinner in his sins, He deprives him of the existence which his transgressions have forfeited and of which he has proved himself unworthy. Says an inspired writer: 'Yet a little while, and the wicked shall not be: yea, thou shalt diligently consider his place, and it shall not be.' And another declares: 'They shall be as though they had not been.' *Psalm 37:10; Obadiah 16.* Covered with infamy, they sink into hopeless, eternal oblivion.

"Thus will be made an end of sin, with all the woe and ruin which have resulted from it. Says the psalmist: 'Thou hast destroyed the wicked, Thou hast put out their name forever and ever. O thou enemy, destructions are come to a perpetual end.' *Psalm 9:5-6.* John, in the revelation, looking forward to the eternal state, hears a universal anthem of praise undisturbed by one note of discord. Every creature in heaven and earth was heard ascribing glory to God. *Revelation 5:13.* There will then be no lost souls to blaspheme God as they writhe in never-ending torment; no wretched beings in hell will mingle their shrieks with the songs of the saved.

"Upon the fundamental error of natural immortality rests the doctrine of consciousness in death—a doctrine, like eternal torment, opposed to the teachings of the Scriptures, to the dictates of reason, and to our feelings of humanity. According to the popular belief, the redeemed in heaven are acquainted with all that takes place on the earth and especially with the lives of the friends whom they have left behind. But how could it be a source of happiness to the dead to know the troubles of the living, to witness the sins committed by their own loved ones, and to see them enduring all the sorrows, disappointments, and anguish of life? How much of heaven's bliss would be enjoyed by those who are hovering over their friends on earth? And how utterly revolting is the belief that as the breath leaves the body the soul of the impenitent is consigned to the flames of hell! To what depths of anguish must those be plunged who see their friends passing to the grave, unprepared to enter upon an eternity of woe and sin! Many have been driven to insanity by this harrowing thought.

"What say the Scriptures concerning these things? David declares that man is not conscious in death. 'His breath goeth forth, he returneth to his earth; in that very day his thoughts perish.' *Psalm 146:4.* Solomon bears the same testimony: 'The living know that they shall die: but the dead know not anything.' 'Their love, and their hatred, and their envy, is now perished; neither have they any more a portion forever in anything that is done under the sun.' 'There is no work, nor device, nor knowledge, nor wisdom, in the grave, whither thou goest.' *Ecclesiastes 9:5-6, 10.*

"When, in answer to his prayer, Hezekiah's life was prolonged fifteen years, the grateful king rendered to God a tribute of praise for His great mercy. In this song, he tells the reason why he thus rejoices: 'The grave cannot praise Thee, death cannot celebrate Thee: they that go down into the pit cannot hope for Thy truth. The living, the living, he shall praise Thee, as I do this day.' *Isaiah 38:18-19.* Popular theology represents the righteous dead as in heaven, entered into bliss and praising God with an immortal tongue, but Hezekiah could see no such glorious prospect in death. With his words agrees the testimony of the psalmist: 'In death there is no remembrance of Thee: in the grave who shall give Thee thanks?' 'The dead praise not the Lord, neither any that go down into silence.' *Psalms 6:5; 115:17.*

"Peter, on the Day of Pentecost, declared that the patriarch David 'is both dead and buried, and his sepulcher is with us onto this day.' 'For David in not ascended into the heavens.' *Acts 2:29, 34.* The fact that David remains in the grave until the resurrection proves that the righteous do not go to heaven at death. It is only through the resurrection, and by virtue of the fact that Christ has risen, that David can at last sit at the right hand of God.

"And said Paul: 'If the dead rise not, then is not Christ raised: and if Christ be not raised, your faith is vain; ye are yet is your sins. Then they also which are fallen asleep in Christ are perished.' *1 Corinthians 15:16-18.* If for four thousand years the righteous had gone directly to heaven at death, how could Paul have said that, if there is no resurrection, 'they also which are fallen asleep in Christ are perished'? No resurrection would be necessary . .

"But when about to leave His disciples, Jesus did not tell them that they would soon come to Him. 'I go to prepare a place for you,' He said. 'And if I go and prepare a place for you, I will come again, and receive you unto myself.' *John 14:2, 3.* And Paul tells us further, that 'the Lord Himself shall descend from heaven with a shout, with the voice of the Archangel, and the trump of God: and the dead in Christ shall rise first: then we which are alive and remain shall be caught up together with them in the clouds, to meet the Lord in the air: and so shall we ever be with the Lord.' And he adds: 'Comfort one another with these words.' *1 Thessalonians 4:16-18* . .

Additional Facts about Halloween

"Before any can enter the mansions of the blessed, their cases must be investigated, and their characters and their deeds must pass in review before God. All are to be judged according to the things written in the books and to be rewarded as their works have been. This judgement does not take place at death. Mark the words of Paul: 'He hath appointed a day, in the which He will judge the world in righteousness by that Man whom He hath ordained, whereof He hath given assurance onto all men, in that He hath raised Him from the dead.' Acts 17:31. Here the apostle plainly stated that a specified time, then future, had been fixed upon for the judgement of the world.

"Jude refers to the same period: 'The angels which kept not their first estate, but left their own habitation, He hath reserved in everlasting chains under darkness unto the judgment of the great day.' And, again, he quotes the words of Enoch: 'Behold, the Lord cometh with ten thousands of His saints, to execute judgment upon all.' Jude 6, 14-15. John declares that he 'saw the dead, small and great, stand before God; and the books were opened .. and the dead were judged out of those things which were written in the books.' Revelation 20:12.

"But if the dead are already enjoying the bliss of heaven or writhing in the flames of hell, what need of a future judgment? The teachings of God's Word on these important points are neither obscure nor contradictory; they may be understood by common minds. But what candid mind can see either wisdom or justice in the current theory? Will the righteous, after the investigation of these cases at the judgment, receive the commendation, 'Well done, thou good and faithful servant .. enter thou into the joy of thy Lord,' when they have been dwelling in His presence, perhaps for long ages? Are the wicked summoned, from the place of torment to receive sentence from the judge of all the earth: 'Depart from Me, ye cursed, into everlasting fire'? (Matthew 25:41). Oh, solemn mockery! Shameful impeachment of the wisdom and justice of God ..

"Nowhere in the sacred Scriptures is found the statement that the righteous go to their reward or the wicked to their punishment at death. The patriarchs and prophets have left no such assurance. Christ and His apostles have given no hint of it. The Bible clearly teaches that the dead do not go immediately to heaven. They are represented as sleeping until the resurrection. *1 Thessalonians 4:14; Job 14:10-12.*

"In the very day when the silver cord is loosed and the golden bowl broken *(Ecclesiastes 12:6),* man's thoughts perish. They that go down to the grave are in silence. They know no more of anything that is done under the sun *(Job 14:21).* Blessed rest for the weary righteous! Time, be it long or short, is but a moment to them. They sleep; they are awakened, by the trump of God, to a glorious immortality. 'For the trumpet shall sound, and the dead shall be raised incorruptible .. So when this corruptible shall have put on incorruption, and this mortal shall have put on immortality, then shall be brought to pass the saying that is written, Death is swallowed up in victory.' *1 Corinthians 15:52, 54.* As they are called forth from their deep slumber they begin to think just where they ceased. The last sensation was the pang of death; the last thought, that they were falling beneath the power of the grave. When they arise from the tomb, their first glad thought will be echoed in the triumphal shout: "O death, where is thy sting? O grave, where to thy victory?" *Verse 55* ..

"The doctrine of man's consciousness in death, especially the belief that spirits of the dead return to minister to the living, has prepared the way for modern spirittualism . .

"The fallen angels who do his bidding appear as messengers from the spirit world. While professing to bring the living into communication with the dead, the prince of evil exercises his bewitching influence upon their minds. He has power to bring before men the appearance of their departed friends. The counterfeit is perfect; the familiar look, the words, the tone, are reproduced with marvelous distinctness. Many are comforted with the assurance that their loved ones are enjoying the bliss of heaven, and without suspicion of danger, they give ear 'to seducing spirits, and doctrines of devils.'

"When they have been led to believe that the dead actually return to communicate with them, Satan causes those to appear who went into the grave unprepared. They claim to be happy in heaven and even to occupy exalted positions there, and thus the error is widely taught that no difference is made between the righteous and the wicked. The pretended visitants from the world of spirits sometimes utter cautions and warnings which prove to be correct. Then, as confidence is gained, they present doctrines that directly undermine faith in the Scriptures. With an appearance of deep interest in the well-being of their friends on earth, they insinuate the most dangerous errors. The fact that they state some truths, and are able at times to foretell future events, gives to their statements an appearance of reliability; and their false teachings are accepted by the multitudes as readily, and believed as implicitly, as if they were the most sacred truths of the Bible. The law of God is set aside, the Spirit of grace despised, the blood of the covenant counted an unholy thing. The spirits deny the deity of Christ . . But none need be deceived by the lying claims of spiritualism. God has given the world sufficient light to enable them to discover the snare. As already shown, the theory which forms the very foundation of spiritualism is at war with the plainest statements of Scripture. The Bible declares that the dead know not anything, that their thoughts have perished; they have no part in anything that is done under the sun; they know nothing of the joys or sorrows of those who were dearest to them on earth.

"Furthermore, God has expressly forbidden all pretended communication with departed spirits. In the days of the Hebrews there was a class of people who claimed, as do the spiritualists of today, to hold communication with the dead. But the 'familiar spirits,' as these visitants from other worlds were called, are declared by the Bible to be 'the spirits of devils.' (Compare Numbers 25:1-3, Psalm 106:28, 1 Corinthians 10:20, Revelation 16:14.)

"The work of dealing with familiar spirits was pronounced an abomination to the Lord, and was solemnly forbidden under penalty of death (Leviticus 19:31, 20:27). The very name of witchcraft is now held in contempt. The claim that men can hold intercourse with evil spirits is regarded as a fable of the Dark Ages. But spiritualism, which numbers its converts by hundreds of thousands, yea, by millions, which has made its way into scientific circles, which has invaded churches and has found favor in legislative bodies, and even in the courts of kings—this mammoth deception is but a revival, in a new disguise, of the witchcraft condemned and prohibited of old . .

"There are few who have any just conception of the deceptive power of spiritualism and the danger of coming under its influence. Many tamper with it merely to gratify their curiosity. They have no real faith in it and would be filled with horror at the thought of yielding themselves to the spirits' control. But they venture upon *the forbidden ground, and the mighty destroyer exercises his power upon them against their will. Let them once be induced to submit their minds to his direction, and he holds them captive. It is impossible, in their own strength, to break away from the bewitching, alluring spell. Nothing but the power of God, granted in answer to the earnest prayer of faith, can deliver these ensnared souls.*

"All who indulge sinful traits of character, or willfully cherish a known sin, are inviting the temptations of Satan. They separate themselves from God and from the watchcare of His angels; as the evil one presents his deceptions, they are without defense and fall an easy prey. Those who thus place themselves in his power little realize where their course will end. Having achieved their overthrow, the tempter will employ them as his agents to lure others to ruin.

"Says the prophet Isaiah: 'When they shall say unto you, Seek unto them that have familiar spirits, and unto wizards that peep, and that mutter: should not a people seek unto their God? for the living to the dead? To the law and to the testimony: if they speak not according to this Word, it is because there is no light in them.' Isaiah 8:19, 20. If men had been willing to receive the truth so plainly stated in the Scriptures concerning the nature of man and the state the dead, they would see in the claims and manifestations of spiritualism the working of Satan with power and signs and lying wonders. But rather than yield the liberty so agreeable to the carnal heart, and renounce the sins which they love, multitudes close their eyes to the light and walk straight on, regardless of the warnings, while Satan weaves his snares about them, and they become his prey. 'Because they received not the love of the truth, that they might be saved,' therefore 'God shall send them strong delusion, that they should

believe a lie.' *2 Thessalonians 2:10, 11* ..

"Many will be confronted by the spirits of devils personating beloved relatives or friends and declaring the most dangerous heresies. These visitors will appeal to our tenderest sympathies and will work miracles to sustain their pretensions. We must be prepared to withstand them with the Bible truth, that the dead know not anything and that they who thus appear are the spirits of devils.

"Just before us is 'the hour of temptation, which shall come upon all the world, to try them that dwell upon the earth.' *Revelation 3:10.* All whose faith is not firmly established upon the Word of God will be deceived and overcome. Satan 'works with all deceivableness of unrighteousness' to gain control of the children of men, and his deceptions will continually increase. But he can gain his object only as men voluntarily yield to his temptations. Those who are earnestly seeking a knowledge of the truth and are striving to purify their souls through obedience, thus doing what they can to prepare for the conflict, will find, in the God of truth, a sure defense. 'Because thou hast kept the word of My patience, I also will keep thee' *(verse 10),* is the Saviour's promise. He would sooner send every angel out of heaven to protect His people than leave one soul that trusts in Him to be overcome by Satan.

"The prophet Isaiah brings to view the fearful deception which will come upon the wicked, causing them to count themselves secure from the judgments of God: 'We have made a covenant with death, and with hell are we at agreement; when the overflowing scourge shall pass through, it shall not come unto us: for we have made lies our refuge, and under falsehood have we hid ourselves.' *Isaiah 28:15.* In the class here described are included those who in their stubborn impenitence comfort them-

Additional Facts about Halloween

selves with the assurance that there is to be no punishment for the sinner; that all mankind, it matters not how corrupt, are to be exalted to heaven, to become as the angels of God. But still more emphatically are those making a covenant with death and an agreement with hell, who renounce the truths which Heaven has provided as a defense for the righteous in the day of trouble, and accept the refuge of lies offered by Satan in its stead—the delusive pretentions of spiritualism.

"Marvelous beyond expression is the blindness of the people of this generation. Thousands reject the Word of God as unworthy of belief and with eager confidence they receive the deceptions of Satan. Skeptics and scoffers denounce the bigotry of those who contend for the faith of prophets and apostles, and they divert themselves by holding up to ridicule the solemn declarations of the Scriptures concerning Christ and the plan of salvation, and the retribution to be visited upon the rejecters of the truth. They affect great pity for minds so narrow, weak, and superstitious as to acknowledge the claims of God and obey the requirements of His law. They manifest as much assurance as if, indeed, they had made a covenant with death and an agreement with hell—as if they had erected an impassable, impenetrable, barrier between themselves and the vengeance of God. Nothing can arouse their fears. So fully have they yielded to the tempter, so closely are they united with him, and so thoroughly imbued with his spirit, that they have no power and no inclination to break away from his snare.

"Satan has long been preparing for his final effort to deceive the world. The foundation of his work was laid by the assurance given to Eve in Eden: 'Ye shall not surely die.' 'In the day ye eat thereof, then your eyes shall be opened, and ye shall be as gods, knowing good and evil.' Genesis 3:4, 5. Little by little he has prepared the way *for his masterpiece of deception in the development of spiritualism. He has not yet reached the full accomplishment of his designs; but it will be reached in the last remnant of time. Says the prophet: 'I saw three unclean spirits like frogs . . they are the spirits of devils, working miracles, which go forth unto the kings of the earth and of the whole world, to gather them to the battle of that great day of God Almighty.' Revelation 16:13, 14. Except those who are kept by the power of God, through faith in His Word, the whole world will be swept into the ranks of this delusion. The people are fast being lulled to a fatal security, to be awakened only by the outpouring of the wrath of God.*

"Saith the Lord God: 'Judgment also will I lay to the line, and righteousness to the plummet: and the hail shall sweep away the refuge of lies, and the waters shall overflow the hiding place. And your covenant with death shall be disannulled, and your agreement with hell shall not stand; when the overflowing scourge shall pass through, then ye shall be trodden down by it.' Isaiah 28:17, 18."
—Great Controversy, 533-562

"When Saul inquired for Samuel, the Lord did not cause Samuel to appear to Saul. He saw nothing. Satan was not allowed to disturb the rest of Samuel in the grave, and bring him up in reality to the witch of Endor. God does not give Satan power to resurrect the dead. But Satan's angels assume the form of dead friends, and speak and act like them, that through professed dead friends he can the better carry on his work of deception. Satan knew Samuel well, and he knew how to represent him before the witch of Endor, and to utter correctly the fate of Saul and his sons."
—2 Bible Commentary, 1022

How to Come to Christ and Stay Close to Him

– Part One –
How Can I Come to God?

Nature and revelation alike testify of God's love. It is transgression of God's law—the law of love—that has brought woe and death. Yet even amid the suffering that results from sin, God's love is revealed. "God is love" is written upon every opening bud, upon every spire of springing grass.

Jesus came to live among men to reveal the infinite love of God. Love, mercy, and compassion were revealed in every act of His life; His heart went out in tender sympathy to the children of men. He took man's nature, that He might reach man's wants. The poorest and humblest were not afraid to approach Him. Such is the character of Christ as revealed in His life. This is the character of God.

It was to redeem us that Jesus lived and suffered and died. He became a "Man of Sorrows," that we might be made partakers of everlasting joy. But this great sacrifice was not made in order to create in the Father's heart a love for man, nor make Him willing to save. No, no! "God so loved the world, that He gave His only-begotten Son." *John 3:16*. The Father loves us, not because of the great propitiation, but He provided the propitiation because He loves us. None but the Son of God could accomplish our

*Summary of all the key points in the book,
Steps to Christ, in the author's own words.*

redemption.

What a value this places upon man! Through transgression the sons of man become subjects of Satan. Through faith in the atoning sacrifice of Christ the sons of Adam may become the sons of God. The matchless love of God for a world that did not love Him! The thought has a subduing power upon the soul and brings the mind into captivity to the will of God.

Man was originally endowed with noble powers and a well-balanced mind. He was perfect in his being, and in harmony with God. His thoughts were pure, his aims holy. But through disobedience, his powers were perverted, and selfishness took the place of love. His nature became so weakened through transgression that it was impossible for him, in his own strength, to resist the power of evil.

It is impossible for us, of ourselves, to escape from the pit of sin in which we are sunken. Our hearts are evil, and we cannot change them. There must be a power working from within, a new life from above, before men can be changed from sin to holiness. That power is Christ. His grace alone can quicken the lifeless faculties of the soul, and attract it to God, to holiness. To all, there is but one answer, "Behold the Lamb of God, which taketh away the sin of the world" (John 1:29). Let us avail ourselves of the means provided for us that we may be transformed into His likeness, and be restored to fellowship with the ministering angels, to harmony and communion with the Father and the Son.

How shall a man be just with God? How shall the sinner be made righteous? It is only through Christ that we can be brought into harmony with God, with holiness; but how are we to come to Christ?

Repentance includes sorrow for sin and a turning away from it. We shall not renounce sin unless we see its sinfulness; until we turn away from it in heart, there will be no real change in the life.

But when the heart yields to the influence of the Spirit of God, the conscience will be quickened and the sinner

How to Come Close to Christ

will discern something of the depth and sacredness of God's holy law, the foundation of His government in heaven and on earth. Conviction takes hold upon the mind and heart.

The prayer of David, after his fall, illustrates the nature of true sorrow for sin. His repentance was sincere and deep. There was no effort to palliate his guilt; no desire to escape the judgment threatened, inspired his prayer. David saw the enormity of his transgression; he saw the defilement of his soul; he loathed his sin. It was not for pardon only that he prayed, but for purity of heart. He longed for the joy of holiness, to be restored to harmony and communion with God. A repentance such as this is beyond the reach of our own power to accomplish; it is obtained only from Christ.

Christ is ready to set us free from sin, but He does not force the will. If we refuse, what more can He do? Study God's Word prayerfully. As you see the enormity of sin, as you see yourself as you really are, do not give up in despair. It was sinners that Christ came to save. When Satan comes to tell you that you are a great sinner, look to your Redeemer and talk of His merits. Acknowledge your sin, but tell the enemy that "Christ came into the world to save sinners" and that you may be saved (1 Tim. 1:15).

"He that covereth his sins shall not prosper: but whoso confesseth and forsaketh them shall have mercy." *Proverbs 28:13*. The conditions of obtaining the mercy of God are simple and just and reasonable. Confess your sins to God, who only can forgive them, and your faults to one another. Those who have not humbled their souls before God in acknowledging their guilt, have not yet fulfilled the first step of acceptance. We must be willing to humble our hearts and comply with the conditions of the Word of truth. The confession that is the outpouring of the inmost soul finds its way to the God of infinite pity. True confession is always of a specific character and acknowledges particular sins. All confession should be definite and to the point. It is written, "If we confess our sins, He is faithful and just to forgive us our sins, and to cleanse us from all unrighteousness" (1 John 1:9).

God's promise is, "Ye shall seek Me, and find Me, when ye shall search for Me with all your heart." *Jeremiah 29:13*. The whole heart must be yielded, or the change can never be wrought in us by which we are to be restored to His likeness.

The warfare against self is the greatest battle that was ever fought. The yielding of self, surrendering all to the will of God, requires a struggle; but the soul must submit to God before it can be renewed in holiness.

In giving ourselves to God, we must necessarily give up all that would separate us from Him. There are those who profess to serve God while they rely upon their own efforts to obey His law, to form a right character, and secure salvation. Their hearts are not moved by any deep sense of the love of Christ, but they seek to perform the duties of the Christian life as that which God requires of them in order to gain heaven. Such religion is worthless.

When Christ dwells in the heart, the soul will be so filled with His love, with the joy of communion with Him, that it will cleave to Him; and in the contemplation of Him, self will be forgotten. Love to Christ will be the spring of action. Such do not ask for the lowest standard, but aim at perfect conformity to the will of their Redeemer.

Do you feel that it is too great a sacrifice to yield all to Christ? Ask yourself the question, "What has Christ given for me?" The Son of God gave all—life and love and suffering—for our redemption. And can it be that we, the unworthy objects of so great love, will withhold our hearts from Him? What do we give up, when we give all? A sin-polluted heart, for Jesus to purify, to cleanse by His own blood, and to save by His matchless love. And yet men think it hard to give up all! God does not require us to give up anything that it is for our best interest to retain. In all that He does, He has the well-being of His children in view.

Many are inquiring, "*How* am I to make the surrender of myself to God?" You desire to give yourself to Him, but you are weak in moral power, in slavery to doubt, and controlled by the habits of your life of sin. Your promises and resolutions are like ropes of sand. You cannot control your thoughts, your impulses, your affections. The knowledge of your broken promises and forfeited pledges weakens your confidence in your own sincerity, and causes you to feel that God cannot accept you; but you need not despair.

What you need to understand is the true force of the will. This is the governing power in the nature of man, the power of decision, or of choice. Everything depends on the right action of the will. The power of choice God has given to men; it is theirs to exercise. You cannot change your heart, you cannot of yourself give to God its affections; but you can *choose* to serve Him. You can give Him your will; He will then work in you to will and to do according to His good pleasure. Thus your whole nature will be brought under the control of the Spirit of Christ; your affections will be centered upon Him, your thoughts will be in harmony with Him.

Desires for goodness and holiness are right as far as they go; but if you stop here, they will avail nothing. Many will be lost while hoping and desiring to be Christians. They do not come to the point of yielding the will to God. They do not *now choose* to be Christians.

Through the right exercise of the will, an entire change may be made in your life. You will have strength from above to hold you steadfast, and thus through constant surrender to God you will be enabled to live the new life, even the life of faith.

As your conscience has been quickened by the Holy Spirit, you have seen something of the evil of sin, of its power, its guilt, its woe; and you look upon it with abhorrence. It is peace that you need. You have confessed your sins, and in heart put them away. You have resolved to give yourself to God. Now go to Him and ask that He will wash away your sins and give you a new heart.

Then believe that He does this *because He has promised*. The gift which God promises us, we must believe we do receive, and it is ours. You are a sinner. You cannot atone for your past sins; you cannot change your heart and make yourself holy. But God promises to do all this for you through Christ. You *believe* that promise. You confess your sins and give yourself to God. You will to serve Him. Just as surely as you do this, God will fulfill His Word to you. If you believe the promise—God supplies the fact. Do not wait to *feel* that you are made whole, but say, "I believe it; it is so, not because I feel it, but because God promised."

—*Summary of all the key points in Steps to Christ, pp. 9-51, in the author's own words.*

– Part Two –
How Can I Remain True to God?

Jesus says, "What things soever ye desire, when ye pray, believe that ye receive them, and ye shall have them" (Mark 11:24). There is a condition to this promise—that we pray according to the will of God. But it is the will of God to cleanse us from sin, to make us His children, and to enable us to live a holy life. So we may ask for these blessings, and believe that we receive them, and thank God that we *have* received them.

Henceforth you are not your own; you are bought with a price. Through this simple act of believing God, the Holy Spirit has begotten a new life in your heart. You are a child born into the family of God, and He loves you as He loves His Son.

Now that you have given yourself to Jesus, do not draw back, do not take yourself away from Him, but day by day say, "I am Christ's; I have given myself to Him"; and ask Him to give you His Spirit and keep you by His grace. As it is by giving yourself to God, and believing Him, that you become His child, so you are to live in Him.

Here is where thousands fail; they do not believe that Jesus pardons them personally, individually. They do not take God at His Word. It is the privilege of all who comply with the conditions to know for themselves that pardon is freely extended for every sinner. Put away the suspicion that God's promises are not meant for you. They are for every repentant transgressor.

Look up, you that are doubting and trembling; for Jesus lives to make intercession for us. Thank God for the gift of His dear Son.

"If any man be in Christ, he is a new creature: old things are passed away; behold, all things are become new." *2 Corinthians 5:17.*

A person may not be able to tell the exact time or place, or trace all the chain of circumstances in the process of conversion; but this does not prove him to be unconverted. A change will be seen in the character, the habits, the pursuits. The contrast will be clear and decided between what they have been and what they have become. Who has the heart? With whom are our thoughts? Of whom do we love to converse? Who has our warmest affections and our best energies? If we are Christ's, our thoughts are with Him. There is no evidence of genuine repentance unless it works reformation. The loveliness of the character of Christ will be seen in His followers. It was His delight to do the will of God.

There are two errors against which the children of God especially need to guard: The first is that of looking to their own works, trusting to anything they can do, to bring themselves into harmony with God. All that man can do without Christ is polluted with selfishness and sin. It is the grace of Christ alone, through faith, which can make us holy.

The opposite and no less dangerous error is that belief in Christ releases men from keeping the law of God; that since by faith alone we become partakers of the grace of Christ, our works have nothing to do with our redemption.

Obedience is the fruit of faith. Righteousness is defined by the standard of God's holy law, as expressed in the ten commandments (Ex 20:3-20). That so-called faith in Christ, which professes to release men from the obligation of obedience to God, is not faith, but presumption. The condition of eternal life is now just what it always has been—just what it was in paradise before the fall of our first parents—perfect obedience to the law of God, perfect righteousness. If eternal life were granted on any condition short of this, then the happiness of the whole universe would be imperiled. The way would be open for sin, with all its train of woe and misery, to be immortalized.

Christ changes the heart. He abides in your heart by faith. You are to maintain this connection with Christ by faith and the continual surrender of your will to Him; and so long as you do this, He will work in you to will and to do according to His good pleasure.

The closer you come to Jesus, the more faulty you will appear in your own eyes; for your vision will be clearer. This is evidence that Satan's delusions are losing their power. No deep-seated love for Jesus can dwell in the heart that does not realize its own sinfulness. The soul that is transformed by the grace of Christ will admire His character. A view of our sinfulness drives us to Him who can pardon; and when the soul, realizing its helplessness, reaches out after Christ, He will reveal Himself in power. The more our sense of need drives us to Him and to the Word of God, the more exalted views we shall have of His character, and the more fully we shall reflect His image.

The change of heart by which we become children of God is in the Bible spoken of as birth. Again it is compared to the germination of the good seed sown by the husbandman. It is God who brings the bud to bloom and the flower to fruit. It is by His power that the seed develops.

As the flower turns to the sun, that the bright beams may aid in perfecting its beauty and symmetry, so should we turn to the Sun of Righteousness, that heaven's light may shine upon us, that our character may be developed into the likeness of Christ.

Do you ask, "How am I to abide in Christ?" In the same way as you received Him at first. "As ye have therefore received Christ Jesus the Lord, so walk in Him." *Colossians 2:6*. By faith you became Christ's, and by faith

How to Remain Close to Christ

you are to grow up in Him—by giving and taking. You are to give all—your heart, your will, your service—give yourself to Him to obey all His requirements; and you must take all—Christ, the fullness of all blessing, to abide in your heart, to be your strength, your righteousness, your everlasting helper—to give you power to obey.

Consecrate yourself to God in the morning; make this your very first work. Let your prayer be, "Take me, O Lord, as wholly Thine. I lay all my plans at Thy feet. Use me today in Thy service. Abide with me, and let all my work be wrought in Thee." This is a daily matter. Each morning consecrate yourself to God for that day. Surrender all your plans to Him, to be carried out or given up as His providence shall indicate. Thus day by day you may be giving your life into the hands of God, and thus your life will be molded more and more after the life of Christ.

A life in Christ is a life of restfulness. There may be no ecstasy of feeling, but there should be an abiding, peaceful trust. When the mind dwells upon self, it is turned away from Christ, the source of strength and life. Hence, it is Satan's constant effort to keep the attention diverted from the Saviour and thus prevent the union and communion of the soul with Christ.

When Christ took human nature upon Him, He bound humanity to Himself by a tie of love that can never be broken by any power save the choice of man himself. Satan will constantly present allurements to induce us to break this tie—to choose to separate ourselves from Christ. But let us keep our eyes fixed upon Christ, and He will preserve us. Looking unto Jesus, we are safe. Nothing can pluck us out of His hand. All that Christ was to the disciples, He desires to be to His children today.

Jesus prayed for us, and He asked that we might be one with Him, even as He is one with the Father. What a union is this! Thus, loving Him and abiding in Him, we shall "grow up into Him in all things, which is the head, even Christ" (Ephesians 4:15).

God is the source of life and light and joy to the universe. Wherever the life of God is in the hearts of men, it will flow out to others in love and blessing.

Our Saviour's joy was in the uplifting and redemption of fallen men. For this He counted not His life dear to Himself, but endured the cross, despising the shame. When the love of Christ is enshrined in the heart, like sweet fragrance it cannot be hidden. Love to Jesus will be manifested in a desire to work as He worked for the blessing and uplifting of humanity. It will lead to love, tenderness, and sympathy toward all the creatures of our heavenly Father's care. Those who are the partakers of the grace of Christ will be ready to make any sacrifice, that others for whom He died may share the heavenly gift. They will do all they can to make the world better for their stay in it. This spirit is the sure outgrowth of a soul truly converted. No sooner does one come to Christ than there is born in his heart a desire to make known to others what a precious friend he has found in Jesus. If we have tasted and seen that the Lord is good, we shall have something to tell. We shall seek to present to others the attractions of Christ and the unseen realities of the world to come. There will be an intensity of desire to follow in the path that Jesus trod.

And the effort to bless others will react in blessings upon ourselves. Those who thus become participants in labors of love are brought nearest to their Creator. The spirit of unselfish labor for others gives depth, stability, and Christlike loveliness to the character, and brings peace and happiness to its possessor. Strength comes by exercise. We need not go to heathen lands, or even leave the narrow circle of the home, if it is there that our duty lies, in order to work for Christ. With a loving spirit we may perform life's humblest duties "unto the Lord" (Colosssians 3:23). If the love of God is in the heart, it will be manifested in the life. You are not to wait for great occasions or to expect extraordinary abilities before you go to work for God. The humblest and poorest of the disciples of Jesus can be a blessing to others.

Many are the ways in which God is seeking to make

Himself known to us and bring us into communion with Him. If we will but listen, Nature speaks to our senses without ceasing. God's created works will teach us precious lessons of obedience and trust.

No tears are shed that God does not notice. There is no smile that He does not mark. If we would but fully believe this, all undue anxieties would be dismissed. Our lives would not be so filled with disappointment as now; for everything, whether great or small, would be left in the hands of God.

God speaks to us through His providential works and through the influence of His Spirit upon the heart. God speaks to us in His Word. Here we have in clearer lines the revelation of His character, of His dealings with men, and the great work of redemption. Fill the whole heart with the words of God. They are the living water, quenching your burning thirst. They are the living bread from heaven.

The theme of redemption is one that the angels desire to look into; it will be the science and the song of the redeemed throughout the ceaseless ages of eternity. Is it not worthy of careful thought and study now? As we meditate upon the Saviour, there will be a hungering and thirsting of soul to become like Him whom we adore.

The Bible was written for the common people. The great truths necessary for salvation are made as clear as noonday. There is nothing more calculated to strengthen the intellect than the study of the Scriptures. But there is little benefit derived from a hasty reading of the Bible. One passage studied, until its significance is clear to the mind and its relation to the plan of salvation is evident, is of more value than the perusal of many chapters with no definite purpose in view and no positive instruction gained.

Keep your Bible with you. As you have opportunity, read it; fix the texts in your memory.

We cannot obtain wisdom without earnest attention and prayerful study. Never should the Bible be studied without prayer. Before opening its pages, we should ask for the enlightenment of the Holy Spirit, and it will be given. Angels from the world of light will be with those who in humility of heart seek for divine guidance. How must God esteem the human race, since He gave His Son to die for them and appoints His Holy Spirit to be man's teacher and continual guide!

Through nature and revelation, through His providence, and by the influence of His Spirit, God speaks to us. But these are not enough; we need also to pour out our hearts to Him. In order to commune with God, we must have something to say to Him concerning our actual life.

Prayer is the opening of the heart to God as to a friend. Not that it is necessary in order to make known to God what we are, but in order to enable us to receive Him. Prayer does not bring God down to us, but brings us up to Him.

Our heavenly Father waits to bestow upon us the fullness of His blessing. What a wonder it is that we pray so little! God is ready and willing to hear the sincere prayer of the humblest of His children. What can the angels of heaven think of poor helpless human beings who are subject to temptation, when God's heart of infinite love yearns toward them, ready to give them more than they can ask or think, and yet they pray so little and have so little faith?

The darkness of the evil one encloses those who neglect to pray. The whispered temptations of the enemy entice them to sin; and it is all because they do not make use of prayer. Yet prayer is the key in the hand of faith to unlock heaven's storehouse, where are treasured the boundless resources of Omnipotence.

There are certain conditions upon which we may expect that God will hear and answer our prayers:

One is that we feel our need of help from Him. If we regard iniquity in our hearts, if we cling to any known sin, the Lord will not hear us; but the prayer of the penitent, contrite soul is always accepted. When all known wrongs are righted, we may believe that God will answer our petitions.

Another element of prevailing prayer is faith. When

our prayers seem not to be answered, we are to cling to the promise; for the time of answering will surely come, and we shall receive the blessing we need most. But to claim that prayer will always be answered in the very way and for the particular thing that we desire, is presumption.

When we come to God in prayer, we should have a spirit of love and forgiveness in our own hearts.

Perseverance in prayer has been made a condition of receiving. We must pray always if we would grow in faith and experience.

We should pray in the family circle, and above all we must not neglect secret prayer, for this is the life of the soul. Family or public prayer alone is not sufficient. Secret prayer is to be heard only by the prayer-hearing God.

There is no time or place in which it is inappropriate to offer up a petition to God. In the crowds of the street, in the midst of a business engagement, we may send up a petition to God and plead for divine guidance.

Let the soul be drawn out and upward, that God may grant us a breath of the heavenly atmosphere. We may keep so near to God that in every unexpected trial our thoughts will turn to Him as naturally as the flower turns to the sun. Keep your wants, your joys, your sorrows, your cares, and your fears before God. You cannot burden Him; you cannot weary Him. He is not indifferent to the wants of His children.

We sustain a loss when we neglect the privilege of associating together to strengthen and encourage one another in the service of God. If Christians would associate together, speaking to each other of the love of God and the precious truths of redemption, their own hearts would be refreshed and they would refresh one another.

We must gather about the cross. Christ and Him crucified should be the theme of contemplation, of conversation, and of our most joyful emotion. We should keep in our thoughts every blessing we receive from God, and when we realize His great love we should be willing to trust everything to the hand that was nailed to the cross for us.

The soul may ascend nearer heaven on the wings of praise. As we express our gratitude, we are approximating to the worship of the heavenly hosts.

Many are at times troubled with the suggestions of skepticism. God never asks us to believe, without giving sufficient evidence upon which to base our faith. Disguise it as they may, the real cause of doubt and skepticism, in most cases, is the love of sin. We must have a sincere desire to know the truth and a willingness of heart to obey it.

—Summary of Steps to Christ, pages 51 to 111, in the author's own words.

"Whoso putteth his trust in the Lord shall be safe."
—Proverbs 29:25

"Fear thou not; for I am with thee."
—Isaiah 41:10

"The joy of the Lord is your strength."
—Nehemiah 8:10

"This God is our God for ever and ever; He will be our guide even unto death."
—Psalm 48:14

"They cry unto the Lord in their trouble, and He saveth them out of their distresses." —Psalm 107:19

"My God shall supply all your need according to His riches in glory by Christ Jesus." —Philippians 4:19

"In all thy ways acknowledge Him, and He shall direct thy paths."
—Proverbs 3:6

Entering a Deeper Walk with God

In this book, we have learned that many gems of truths were lost in the Dark Ages, which we must recover today. One of the most precious is the fact that you can have a far closer walk with God than you imagined possible.

When we study God's Word—the Holy Bible—and obey its truths, we are able to enter upon the path of obedience that God invites us to enter.

In this chapter you will discover what the Scriptures say about a special truth that God has for you —

FACT NUMBER ONE—The Sabbath was given to all mankind at the Creation of this world.

The seventh-day Sabbath was given to mankind on the seventh day of Creation Week.

"Thus the heavens and the earth were finished, and all the host of them. And on the seventh day God ended His work which He had made; and He rested on the seventh day from all His work which He had made.

"And God blessed the seventh day, and sanctified it: because that in it He had rested from all His work which God created and made."—*Genesis 2:1-3*.

God dedicated and set aside the Sabbath as a rest day—2,000 years before the first Jew. Abraham is considered by all to have been the first Jew. He lived about 2000 B.C. Biblical records indicate that the Creation of this world took place about 4000 B.C. So the Bible Sabbath is not Jewish! It is for mankind; it is for all the world.

"The Sabbath was made for man."—*Mark 2:27*.

FACT NUMBER TWO—The Sabbath is a memorial of Creation and our salvation.

First, it is a memorial of Creation.

"It is a sign between Me and the children of Israel for ever: for in six days the Lord made heaven and earth, and on the seventh day He rested, and was refreshed."—*Exodus 31:17.*

As a memorial of the Creation of this world, the Sabbath cannot pass away without first having this world pass away—and creating a new one! Our planet could not have a new or different Sabbath day, without having it first hurled into oblivion—and then a new planet created from nothing. But no such event has occurred.

Second, the Sabbath is a symbol of our salvation. When we keep it, we tell all the world that we belong to God and that we serve and obey Him. The seventh-day Sabbath is a sign of our conversion, sanctification, and salvation:

"Verily My Sabbaths ye shall keep: for it is a sign between Me and you throughout your generations; that ye may know that I am the Lord that doth sanctify you."—*Exodus 31:13.*

"Moreover also I gave them My Sabbaths to be a sign between Me and them, that they might know that I am the Lord that sanctify them."—*Ezekiel 20:12.*

"And hallow My Sabbaths; and they shall be a sign between Me and you, that ye may know that I am the Lord your God."—*Ezekiel 20:20.*

But what about Christ's resurrection? Nowhere in Scripture are we told to keep any day in honor of Christ's resurrection. To do so is unscriptural. On the contrary, to set aside the Creation and sanctification Sabbath of the Bible—for another day of the week—and excuse it by saying that we do so "in honor of Christ's resurrection"—is indeed to do a very daring thing. Who dare presume to set aside the Memorial of Creation and salvation for any reason! To knowingly do so flies in the face of repeated, direct, Biblical commands by the God of heaven. To do so denies that He is our Creator and Redeemer.

If we abandon the Bible Sabbath and keep another day holy, in the Judgment what excuse can we offer? There is no Bible reason for keeping the first day of the week holy instead of the seventh day.

Entering a Deeper Walk with God

FACT NUMBER THREE—The people of God kept the Bible Sabbath before the Ten Commandments were given at Mount Sinai.

The Sabbath Truth was first given to our race in Eden before the fall of man. It was given before sin existed. It was given to every man to link him to his God. And if Adam needed the Sabbath, we need it all the more today.

God's people had it before Mount Sinai. Four chapters before the Ten Commandments were given on Mount Sinai, the God of heaven spoke in such a way that it is obvious that the seventh-day Sabbath was already well-known by the people of God—but not always well-kept. Read Exodus 16.

There are those who say that the seventh-day Sabbath was not commanded by God, nor kept by man before it was spoken from Mount Sinai in Exodus 20. But Genesis 2:1-3 and Exodus 16 prove otherwise.

FACT NUMBER FOUR—The seventh-day Sabbath Commandment lies in the very heart of the Moral Law of Ten Commandments.

"Remember The Sabbath day, to keep it holy.

"Six days shalt thou labour, and do all thy work. But the seventh day is the Sabbath of the Lord thy God: in it thou shalt not do any work, thou, nor thy son, nor thy daughter, thy manservant, nor thy maidservant, nor thy cattle, nor thy stranger that is within thy gates.

"For in six days the Lord made heaven and earth, the sea, and all that in them is, and rested the seventh day: wherefore the Lord blessed the Sabbath day, and hallowed it."—*Exodus 20:8-11.*

The Sabbath Commandment is part of the Moral Law of Ten Commandments. The Apostle James tells us that if we break any part of this law, we have broken it all (James 2:10-12). We cannot tear out the Fourth Commandment without setting aside all the others as well. They all stand together, because the God of Heaven put them all together.

We do not decide which day of the week is to be kept holy unto God; He alone is to do this. It is for Him to command; it is for us to obey.

Some say that Genesis 2:1-3 is not a command for man to keep the Sabbath, and therefore we do not obey it. But Exodus 16 and 20 clearly show that man *is* commanded to keep it holy. And who dare say that the Ten Commandments were only for the Jewish race? Are the rest of us permitted to lie, steal, cheat, and commit adultery? Are only the Hebrews to observe these ten moral principles?

The reason for the commandment is the Creation of this world: "For in six days the Lord made heaven and earth." This is not something local, merely for a Semitic race—it is a commandment for all in the entire world who shall bow down and worship their Creator in humble thankfulness for His plan to save them through the life and death of Jesus Christ. It was given at the Creation of this world, and was given to every man, woman, and child who shall live on this planet.

God wrote these Ten Commandments with His own finger (Ex 31:18, Deut 9:10). He wrote them on the most enduring thing in the world, and that is rock (Ex 31:18). And He wishes to write them also on our hearts.

"This is the covenant that I will make with them after those days, saith the Lord: I will put My laws into their hearts, and in their minds will I write them."—*Hebrews 10:16 (Heb 8:10, Jer 31:33).*

And, if we will let Him, through the New Covenant He will write His holy law upon our hearts. To have the Ten Commandments written on our hearts means two things: First, a willingness to obey them and, second, letting God enable us to do so by the grace of Jesus, His Son. Obedience to God's law is to become an integral part of our lives.

FACT NUMBER FIVE—The weekly seventh-day Sabbath is part of the Moral Law contained in the Ten Commandments. It will stand forever. The yearly sabbaths were part of the ceremonial laws that prefigured, or foreshadowed, the death and ministry of Christ.

These "shadow laws," such as Passover and the Wave Sheaf which were a part of the ceremonial or sacrificial law, would not endure past the death of Christ.

"For the [ceremonial] law having a shadow of good things to come, and not the very image of the things, can never with

Entering a Deeper Walk with God

those sacrifices which they offered year by year continually make the comers thereunto perfect. For then would they not have ceased to be offered? . . But in those sacrifices there is a remembrance again made of sins every year. For it is not possible that the blood of bulls and of goats should take away sins."—*Hebrews 10:1-4.*

These ceremonial laws were not written on rock, but were contained in ordinances and written on parchment. The rock was to endure, but the ordinances that foreshadowed the death of Christ were to pass away at His death. It is for this reason that we do not today observe the yearly sabbaths of the Passover and the Wave Sheaf.

"Blotting out the handwriting of ordinances that was against us, which was contrary to us, and took it out of the way, nailing it to His cross . . Let no man therefore judge you in meat, or in drink, or in respect of an holyday, or of the new moon, or of the sabbath days. Which are a shadow of things to come; but the body is of Christ."—*Colossians 2:14,16-17.*

In the Greek it says, "or of the sabbaths." **There is one weekly Sabbath; it comes down to us from the Creation of this world and will be kept in the New Earth (Isa. 66:22-23). But the yearly sabbaths did not begin until Moses.** They foreshadowed and explained the coming death of Christ till it happened; and, at His death, they were nailed to His cross.

If the ordinances containing the yearly sabbaths had not been set aside at Calvary, we would need now to sacrifice animals on various occasions throughout the year. But we are not now to slay lambs; for Christ, our Passover Lamb, has been sacrificed for us.

"Behold the Lamb of God, which taketh away the sin of the world."—*John 1:29.*

"For even Christ our Passover is sacrificed for us."—*1 Corinthians 5:7.*

FACT NUMBER SIX—**Christ's disciples faithfully kept the Bible Sabbath, not Sunday.**

The disciples had been with Jesus for three and a half years, and had listened closely to His teachings. What they did at the time of His death on Calvary shows what He taught them. The sacred importance of the seventh-day Sabbath was of such concern to them that they would not even prepare the body of Jesus properly for burial on Friday, lest they transgress the Fourth Commandment.

"And now when the even was come, because it was the preparation, that is, the day before the Sabbath . . Mary Magdalene and Mary the mother of Joses beheld where He was laid.

"And when the Sabbath was past, Mary Magdalene, and Mary the mother of James, and Salome, had bought sweet spices, that they might come and anoint Him. And very early in the morning the first day of the week, they came unto the sepulchre at the rising of the sun. And they said among themselves, Who shall roll us away the stone from the door of the sepulchre?"—*Mark 15:42, 47-16:3.*

For more on this, read Luke 23:53-24:2.

FACT NUMBER SEVEN—According to the New Testament, the Apostles of Jesus always kept the Bible Sabbath.

The Apostles kept the Bible Sabbath (Acts 13:14, 42; 16:13; 17:1-2).

Paul supported himself by tentmaking; and then, on the Sabbath, he would preach the gospel.

"Because he was of the same craft, he abode with them, and wrought: for by their occupation, they were tentmakers. And he reasoned in the synagogue every Sabbath, and persuaded the Jews and the Greeks . . He continued there a year and six months, teaching the Word of God among them."—*Acts 18:3-4, 11.*

Paul's manner was the same as Christ's custom: to keep the Bible Sabbath (Acts 17:1-2, Luke 4:16).

Paul never taught that the Moral Law was, or could be, set aside. It will ever govern the conduct of mankind.

"Do we then make void the law through faith? God forbid: yea, we establish the law."—*Romans 3:31.*

"What shall we say then? Shall we continue in sin, that grace may abound? God forbid. How shall we, that are dead to

Entering a Deeper Walk with God

sin, live any longer therein?"—*Romans 6:1-2.*

"What shall we say then? Is the law sin? God forbid. Nay, I had not known sin, but by the law: for I had not known lust, except the law had said, Thou shalt not covet."—*Romans 7:7.*

Paul clearly saw that the problem was that we needed to obey the law; there was nothing wrong with the requirements of the law itself.

"Wherefore the law is holy, and the commandment holy, and just, and good."—*Romans 7:12.*

"Circumcision is nothing, and uncircumcision is nothing, but [that which is important is] the keeping of the commandments of God."—*1 Corinthians 7:19.*

The moral standard that governs mankind was not relaxed or destroyed by the death of Christ; for, indeed, it is through the merits of Christ's sacrifice that we can be empowered to keep that law.

"Thou shalt call His name Jesus, for He shall save His people from their sins."—*Matthew 1:21.*

Jesus saves us from our sins, not in our sins. And since sin is the breaking of the Ten Commandments, it is obvious that He saves us by enabling us, strengthening us, to keep that law.

"Whosoever committeth sin transgresseth also the law: for sin is the transgression of the law."—*1 John 3:4.*

The other Apostles saw this same great truth, that the moral standard that governs mankind was not relaxed or destroyed by the death of Christ:

"But be ye doers of the Word, and not hearers only, deceiving your own selves. For if any be a hearer of the Word, and not a doer, he is like unto a man beholding his natural face in a glass. For he beholdeth himself, and goeth his way, and straightway forgetteth what manner of man he was.

"But whoso looketh into the perfect law of liberty, and continueth therein, he being not a forgetful hearer, but a doer of the work, this man shall be blessed in his deed . . For whosoever shall keep the whole law, and yet offend in one point, he is guilty of all. For He that saith, Do not commit adultery, said also, Do not kill. Now if thou commit no adultery, yet if thou kill, thou art become a transgressor of the law. So speak ye, and so do, as they that shall be judged by the law of liberty .. Faith, if it hath not works, is dead, being alone. Yea, a man may say, Thou hast faith, and I have works; shew me thy faith without thy works, and I will shew thee my faith by my works."—*James 1:22-25; 2:10-12, 17-18.*

"By this we know that we love the children of God, when we love God, and keep His commandments. For this is the love of God, that we keep His commandments: and His commandments are not grievous."—*1 John 5:2-3.*

FACT NUMBER EIGHT—God predicted, in Scripture, that men would later try to change the Law of God—and especially the "time law."

The Bible Sabbath is very important—for it is the very center of our worship of God! If men were later to try to change it to another day, we should surely expect a Bible prophecy saying that it would happen.

"And he [the little horn power] shall speak great words against the most High, and shall wear out the saints of the most High, and think to change times and laws: and they shall be given into His hand until a time and times and the dividing of time."—*Daniel 7:25.*

The church of the Dark Ages was to rule the world for 1260 years, and during this time would try to tear out God's holy Time Law and put a counterfeit in its place. Oh, what blasphemy men can dream up, when they are tempted by Satan to gain religious control of their fellow men!

"For that day [the Second Coming of Christ] shall not come, except there come a falling away first, and that man of sin be revealed, the son of perdition; who opposeth and exalteth himself above all that is called God, or that is worshipped."—*2 Thessalonians 2:3-4.*

God said:

"And hallow My Sabbaths; and they shall be a sign between Me and you, that ye may know that I am the Lord your God."—*Ezekiel 20:20.*

After the New Testament was finished and the Apostles had died, men tried to transfer the sacredness from the seventh to the first day of the week. They tried to change the "time law."

Roman Catholic: "It is well to remind the Presbyterians, Baptists, Methodists, and all other Christians, that the Bible does not support them anywhere in their observance of Sunday. Sunday is an institution of the Roman Catholic Church, and those who observe the day observe a commandment of the Catholic Church."—*Priest Brady, in an address at Elizabeth, N.J., March 17, 1903; reported in the Elizabeth N.J. News, March 18, 1903.*

"You may search the Bible from Genesis to Revelation, and you will not find a single line authorizing the sanctification of Sunday. The Scriptures enforce the religious observance of Saterday, a day which we never sanctify."—*Cardinal James Gibbon, The Faith of Our Fathers, chapter 8.*

"If Protestants would follow the Bible, they should worship God on the Sabbath day. In keeping the Sunday they are following a law of the Catholic Church."—*Albert Smith, Chancellor of the Archdiocese of Baltimore, replying for the cardinal, in a letter of February 10, 1920.*

"We hold upon this earth the place of God Almighty."—*Pope Leo XIII, Encyclical Letter, June 20, 1894; The Great Encyclical Letters of Leo XIII, p. 304.*

"Prove to me from the Bible alone that I am bound to keep Sunday holy. There is no such law in the Bible. It is a law of the Holy Catholic Church alone. The Bible says 'Remember the Sabbath day to keep it holy.' The Catholic Church says, No. By my divine power I abolish the Sabbath day and command you to keep holy the first day of the week. And lo! The entire civilized world bows down in reverent obedience to the command of the Holy Catholic Church."—*Priest Thomas Enright, CSSR, President of Redemptorist College, Kansas City, MO, in a lecture at Hartford, Kansas Weekly Call, February 22, 1884, and the American Sentinel, a New York Roman Catholic journal, in June 1893, p. 173.*

"Of course the Catholic Church claims that the change was her act .. AND THE ACT IS A MARK of her ecclesiastical power."—*From the office of Cardinal Gibbons, through Chancellor H.F. Thomas, November 11, 1895.*

How important it is that we obey the commandments of God rather than the commandments of men.

"Know ye not, that to whom ye yield yourselves servants to obey, his servants ye are to whom ye obey?"—*Romans 6:16.*

"It is written, Thou shalt worship the Lord thy God, and Him only shalt thou serve."—*Matthew 4:10.*

"But in vain they do worship Me, teaching for doctrines the commandments of men."—*Matthew 15:9.*

"How long halt ye between two opinions? If the Lord be God, follow Him; but if Baal, then follow him."—*1 Kings 18:21.*

FACT NUMBER NINE—The seventh-day Sabbath, instituted by God at the Creation of this world, is the seal of His governmental authority.

God's basic governmental code for mankind is the Ten Commandments. Of those ten, only the Sabbath commandment reveals the name of our Creator and Lawgiver.

Of all the commandments in the Decalogue, only the Fourth Commandment reveals the (1) name, (2) authority, and (3) dominion of the Author of this Law:

In six days, (1) the Lord (name) (2) made (office—the Creator) (3) heaven and earth (dominion or territory over which He rules). **This commandment alone contains the seal of God.**

Examine the seal of a notary public or any other legal seal. Each seal will always contain the above three identifying marks.

"Remember the Sabbath day, to keep it holy .. for in six days the Lord made heaven and earth, the sea, and all that in them is, and rested the seventh day: wherefore the Lord blessed the Sabbath day, and hallowed it."—*Exodus 20:8, 11.*

The Sabbath commandment contains the seal of God, and the Sabbath itself—given in this commandment—is inseparably connected with this seal. For the Sabbath is the basis of all true worship

Entering a Deeper Walk with God

of our Creator. And this worship lies at the heart of all our acknowledgment of His authority as our Creator and our God. The Sabbath is ever to be kept as a sign that we belong to Him. And the keeping of it brings us within the circle of this seal.

The seal is impressed in order that all may know the authority from whence it comes—and that all may know that it is not to be changed. **The seventh-day Sabbath comes from God. Let no man dare to tamper with it—for the seal of God is upon it.**

"Now, O king, establish the decree, and sign the writing, that it be not changed."—*Daniel 6:8.*

"Bind up the testimony, seal the law among My disciples."—*Isaiah 8:16.*

"It [the Sabbath] is a sign between Me and the children of Israel for ever: for in six days the Lord made heaven and earth, and on the seventh day He rested, and was refreshed."—*Exodus 31:17.*

"And hallow My Sabbaths; and they shall be a sign between Me and you, that ye may know that I am the Lord your *God.*"—*Ezekiel 20:20.*

The Sabbath is a powerful sign of God's creative power—not only of this earth, but within our lives as well. It requires the same power to clean our lives and redeem us as it did to create us in the first place.

"Create in me a clean heart, O God."—*Psalm 51:10.*

"We are . . created in Christ Jesus unto good works."—*Ephesians 2:10.*

The Bible tells us there is to be a special sealing work in these last days, just before the return of Jesus in the clouds of heaven.

"And I saw another angel ascending from the east, having the seal of the living God: and he cried with a loud voice to the four angels . . saying, Hurt not the earth, neither the sea, nor the trees, till we have sealed the servants of our God in their foreheads."—*Revelation 7:2-3 (Eze 9:1-6).*

"And I looked, and, lo, a Lamb stood on the mount Sion, and with Him an hundred forty and four thousand, having His Father's name written in their foreheads."—*Revelation 14:1.*

The name of the Father is expressive of His character. When Moses asked to see the glory of God, the Lord passed by and told His name—that which He was like:

"The Lord, the Lord God, merciful and gracious, longsuffering, and abundant in goodness and truth."—*Exodus 34:6.*

And as we look at God's holy law, we see another view of His character. It is a transcript of that character. It is God's characteristics written on everlasting stone. He wants us to live it out in our lives.

When God writes His name on your forehead and right hand, this means He writes His law on your heart. This is the work of the new covenant (Heb 8:10, 10:16, Jer 31:33); and that work reaches its climax when God "seals in" His own people, just before He returns the second time in the clouds of heaven. What are those sealed ones like? They are fully obedient to the Law of God:

"And in their mouth was found no guile: for they are without fault before the throne of God."—*Revelation 14:5.*

But in the final crisis before His return, there will be a people who will yield obedience to the beast instead of to God.

"And the third angel followed them, saying with a loud voice, If any man worship the beast and his image, and receive his mark in his forehead, or in his hand, the same shall drink of the wine of the wrath of God."—*Revelation 14:9-10.*

"And he [the beast] causeth all, both small and great, rich and poor, free and bond, to receive a mark in their right hand, or in their foreheads."—*Revelation 13:16.*

In contrast with those who serve the beast and receive his mark are those who, in the last days, will serve God and receive His seal. How can they be identified? God has told us in His Word. Here is a description of God's remnant people at the end of time:

"And the dragon [Satan, working through his agents] was wroth with the woman [the true church], and went to make war with the remnant of her seed, which keep the commandments of God, and have the testimony of Jesus Christ."—*Revelation 12:17.*

And the third angel of Revelation 14, which warns men to not receive the mark of the beast, also tells them how to avoid receiving

Entering a Deeper Walk with God

it—by keeping the commandments of God through the faith of Jesus Christ:

"And the third angel followed them, saying with a loud voice, If any man worship the beast and his image, and receive his mark in his forehead, or in his hand, the same shall drink of the wine of the wrath of God, which is poured out without mixture . . Here is the patience of the saints: here are they that keep the commandments of God, and the faith of Jesus."—*Revelation 14:9-10, 12.*

The final crisis will be caused by a decree of the beast, that all men must disobey a commandment of the law of God. The nations and churches of the world will not require men to steal or lie or commit adultery. The growing movement toward national Sunday laws is growing stronger every passing year. It is seen that in this point, and in this alone, will be found the heart of the crisis of Revelation 13 and 14.

The first angel of Revelation 14 calls on all men everywhere, today, to reverence God—by returning to the worship of the Creator of all things.

"And I saw another angel fly in the midst of heaven, having the everlasting gospel to preach unto them that dwell on the earth, and to every nation, and kindred, and tongue, and people.

"Saying with a loud voice, Fear God, and give glory to Him; for the hour of His judgment is come: and worship Him that made heaven, and earth, and the sea, and the fountains of waters."—*Revelation 14:6-7.*

As the crisis nears, we must prepare for it.

"The observance of Sunday by the Protestants is an homage they pay, in spite of themselves, to the authority of the [Catholic] Church."—*Monsignor Louis Segur, Plain Talk About the Protestantism of Today, p. 213.*

Already we are facing Sunday closing laws on local levels. Men are prohibited from doing business on the first working day of the week, lest they be fined or imprisoned. And the situation will grow worse in the days just ahead.

"That the image of the beast should both speak, and cause

[decree] that as many as would not worship the image of the beast should be killed. And he causeth all, both small and great, rich and poor, free and bond, to receive a mark in their right hand, or in their foreheads: and that no man might buy or sell, save he that had the mark."—*Revelation 13:15-17.*

But there is victory for those who will stand true to the God of heaven. There is overcoming power for those who will "keep the commandments of God and the faith of Jesus" (Rev 14:12).

"And I saw . . them that had gotten the victory over the beast, and over his image, and over his mark, and over the number of his name, stand on the sea of glass, having the harps of God."—*Revelation 15:2.*

FACT NUMBER TEN—God's remnant people will keep the Bible Sabbath, and that holy day will be kept throughout eternity.

(1) Even though there are over two thousand denominations today, the remnant people of God, living at the end of time, can be identified. God has identified them for us. After speaking about how the antichrist power in the Dark Ages tried for centuries to destroy the people of God, we are told how to identify them in these last days, just before Christ returns in the clouds for His own:

"And the dragon was wroth with the woman, and went to make war with the remnant of her seed, which keep the commandments of God, and have the testimony of Jesus Christ."—*Revelation 12:17.*

And the third angel, after warning all men against receiving the mark of the beast, tells us clearly who will be the little group that will stand apart from this almost universal apostasy:

"Here is the patience of the saints: here are they that keep the commandments of God, and the faith of Jesus."—*Revelation 14:12.*

It will be an almost universal apostasy. All around us can be seen a rising tide of rebellion against the Ten Commandments. The colleges and universities teach that man is but an animal descended from worms and amoeba. The churches teach that God destroyed the Ten Commandments at Calvary and that Jesus died to take sinners to heaven just as they are. Governmental agencies are relaxing moral

Entering a Deeper Walk with God

restrictions and permitting gambling, abortion, homosexuality, and other vices.

This world is becoming a curse, but soon God will intervene. Prophecy tells us that before the end there will be a small company who will stand true to the commandments of God, by faith in Jesus Christ.

(2) And soon this present evil world will be ended suddenly by the return of Jesus Christ—and heaven will begin for the faithful.

And, in that heaven, the seventh-day Sabbath will be kept forever. God's people suffered and died for it down here, and they will worship God on that holy day through all ages to come.

Revelation 21 and 22 tells us about this new life with Jesus, when sin has come to an end and the wicked are no longer alive.

"And I saw a new heaven and a new earth: for the first heaven and the first earth were passed away; and there was no more sea . . And he shewed me a pure river of water of life, clear as crystal, proceeding out of the throne of God and of the Lamb."—*Revelation 21:1; 22:1.*

And then we are told who will enter that beautiful new world:

"Blessed are they that do His commandments, that they may have right to the tree of life, and may enter in through the gates into the city."—*Revelation 22:14.*

But more: There is the promise that they will keep the holy Sabbath through all eternity.

"For, behold, I create new heavens and a new earth: and the former shall not be remembered, nor come into mind . . And they shall build houses, and inhabit them; and they shall plant vineyards, and eat the fruit of them. They shall not build, and another inhabit; they shall not plant, and another eat: for as the days of a tree are the days of My people, and Mine elect shall long enjoy the work of their hands . . The wolf and the lamb shall feed together, and the lion shall eat straw like the bullock; and dust shall be the serpent's meat. They shall not hurt nor destroy in all My holy mountain, saith the Lord . .

"For as the new heavens and the new earth, which I will make, shall remain before Me, saith the Lord, so shall your seed and your name remain. And it shall come to pass, that from one new moon to another, and from one Sabbath to another, shall all flesh come to worship before Me, saith the Lord."—*Isaiah 65:17, 21-22, 25; 66:22-23.*

Now you have seen God's plan for His people. And it is a wonderful one. It can begin for you right now. And it will continue on throughout eternity. Why not begin today—this very week? Ask God to forgive you for the past, and tell Him that, by His grace, you will worship your Creator on His day! This is the best decision you can make. Go to Him just now. He will help you make it.

And next Sabbath—begin that holy walk with God on His day, the holy day of Isaiah 58. Read that chapter and see the blessings He will add, if you will but let Him take over your life.

But think not that there will be no problems or trials. Satan will bring many upon you. He hates the Sabbath and all who will stand loyal to it. Yet if you will determine to be true to God and His Word, you will have strength from above to go through all that lies ahead.

And one day soon, if faithful to the end, you with the redeemed of all ages will rejoice on the sea of glass and will receive from the hand of Jesus the overcomer's crown. And you will be given that new name, expressive of a new character. And you will begin a walk with Jesus that will last through all eternity to come.

"And one of the elders answered, saying unto me, What are these which are arrayed in white robes? and whence come they?

"And I said unto him, Sir, thou knowest. And he said unto me, These are they which came out of great tribulation, and have washed their robes, and made them white in the blood of the Lamb.

"Therefore are they before the throne of God, and serve Him day and night in His temple: and He that sitteth on the throne shall dwell among them.

"They shall hunger no more, neither thirst any more; neither shall the sun light on them, nor any heat.

"For the Lamb which is in the midst of the throne shall feed them, and shall lead them unto living fountains of waters: and

God shall wipe away all tears from their eyes."—*Revelation 7:13-17.*

THE BIBLE:
DIVINE GUIDANCE FOR YOUR LIFE

What is the purpose of the Bible?

2 Peter 1:21—"For the prophecy came not in old time by the will of man, but holy men of God spake as they were moved by the Holy Ghost."

John 20:30-31—"And many other signs truly did Jesus in the presence of His disciples, which are not written in this book: But these are written, that ye might believe that Jesus is the Christ, the Son of God; and that believing ye might have life through His name."

Psalm 119:11—"Thy Word have I hid in mine heart, that I might not sin against Thee."

Psalm 119:105—"Thy Word is a lamp unto my feet, and a light unto my path."

Romans 15:4—"For whatsoever things were written aforetime were written for our learning, that we through patience and comfort of the Scriptures might have hope."

How should we study the Bible?

Acts 17:11—"These were more noble than those in Thessalonica, in that they received the Word with all readiness of mind, and searched the Scriptures daily, whether those things were so."

Isaiah 28:10—"For precept must be upon precept, precept upon precept; line upon line, line upon line; here a little, and there a little."

2 Timothy 2:15—"Study to show thyself approved unto God, a workman that needeth not to be ashamed, rightly dividing the word of truth."

John 5:39—"Search the Scriptures, for in them ye think ye have eternal life; and they are they which testify of Me."

THE PLAN OF REDEMPTION:
GOD'S PLAN TO SAVE YOU FROM SIN

Romans 3:23—"For all have sinned and come short of the glory of God."

Isaiah 59:2—"But your iniquities have separated between you and your God, and your sins have hid His face from you, that He will not hear."

Romans 6:23—"For the wages of sin is death; but the gift of God is eternal life through Jesus Christ our Lord."

2 Peter 3:9—"The Lord is not slack concerning His promise, as some men count slackness; but is longsuffering to us-ward, not willing that any should perish, but that all should come to repentance."

Exodus 34:6-7—"The Lord God, merciful and gracious, longsuffering, and abundant in goodness and truth, keeping mercy for thousands, forgiving iniquity and transgression and sin, and that will by no means clear the guilty."

John 3:16-20—"For God so loved the world, that He gave His only begotten Son, that whosoever believeth in Him should not perish, but have everlasting life. For God sent not His Son into the world to condemn the world; but that the world through Him might be saved. He that believeth on Him is not condemned: but he that believeth not is condemned already, because he hath not believed in the name of the only begotten Son of God. And this is the condemnation, that light is come into the world, and men loved darkness rather than light, because their deeds were evil. For every one that doeth evil hateth the light, neither cometh to the light, lest his deeds should be reproved."

Luke 19:10—"For the Son of man is come to seek and to save that which was lost."

Matthew 1:21—"He shall save His people from their sins."

Isaiah 53:6—"All we like sheep have gone astray; we have turned every one to his own way; and the Lord hath laid on him the iniquity of us all."

Acts 16:31—"Believe on the Lord Jesus Christ, and thou shalt be saved."

2 Corinthians 6:2—"Now is the accepted time; behold, now is the day of salvation."

Entering a Deeper Walk with God

John 1:12—"But as many as received Him, to them gave He power to become the sons of God, even to them that believe on His name."

Galatians 2:20—"I am crucified with Christ: nevertheless I live; yet not I, but Christ liveth in me: and the life which I now live in the flesh I live by the faith of the Son of God, who loved me, and gave Himself for me."

John 3:3—"Verily, verily, I say unto thee, Except a man be born again, he cannot see the kingdom of God."

2 Corinthians 5:17—"Therefore if any man be in Christ, he is a new creature: old things are passed away; behold, all things are become new."

Philippians 2:13—"For it is God which worketh in you both to will and to do of His good pleasure."

Hebrews 10:16—"I will put My laws into their hearts, and in their minds will I write them."

1 John 1:9—"If we confess our sins, He is faithful and just to forgive us our sins, and to cleanse us from all unrighteousness."

Philippians 4:13—"I can do all things through Christ which strengtheneth me."

OBEDIENCE BY FAITH:
HOW GOD ENABLES YOU TO OBEY HIM

1 - GOD HAS A GOVERNMENT

Psalm 103:19—"The Lord hath prepared His throne in the heavens; and His kingdom ruleth over all."

2 - THERE CAN BE NO GOVERNMENT WITHOUT LAW

Romans 7:12—"The law is holy, and the commandment holy, and just, and good."

Romans 7:14—"For we know that the law is spiritual: but I am carnal, sold under sin."

Proverbs 28:9—"He that turneth away his ear from hearing the law, even his prayer shall be abomination."

3 - GOD'S LAW WAS FOR MEN IN BIBLE TIMES

Romans 3:31—"Do we then make void the law through faith?

God forbid: yea, we establish the law."

James 2:10-12—"For whosoever shall keep the whole law, and yet offend in one point, he is guilty of all. For He that said, Do not commit adultery, said also Do not kill. Now if thou commit no adultery, yet if thou kill, thou art become a transgressor of the law. So speak ye, and so do, as they that shall be judged by the law of liberty."

4 - GOD'S LAW IS FOR THE REMNANT IN THE LAST DAYS

Revelation 12:17—"And the dragon was wroth with the woman, and went to make war with the remnant of her seed, which keep the commandments of God, and have the testimony of Jesus Christ."

Revelation 14:12—"Here is the patience of the saints: here are they that keep the commandments of God, and the faith of Jesus" *(also verses 13-15).*

5 - THERE IS GENERAL REBELLION AGAINST GOD'S LAW

Romans 8:7—"The carnal mind is enmity against God: for it is not subject to the law of God, neither indeed can be."

Psalm 119:126—"It is time for Thee, Lord, to work: for they have made void Thy law."

6 - THERE ARE PROMISES FOR THE OBEDIENT

Psalm 119:165—"Great peace have they which love Thy law: and nothing shall offend them."

Isaiah 48:18—"O that thou hadst hearkened to My commandments! then had thy peace been as a river, and thy righteousness as the waves of the sea."

7 - THE SACRIFICIAL LAWS WERE ABOLISHED AT THE CROSS
(Hebrews 10:1-16)

Colossians 2:14—"Blotting out the handwriting of ordinances that was against us, which was contrary to us, and took it out of the way, nailing it to His cross."

Colossians 2:17—"Which are a shadow of things to come; but the body is of Christ."

8 - WHAT DOES THE LAW DO FOR THE SINNER?

God uses the law to do for the sinner just what needs to be done. The sinner must realize that he is a sinner. The heavy hand of the law must be laid upon him, and he must be arrested in his course. Notice the

Entering a Deeper Walk with God

following carefully:

1. It gives a knowledge of sin.
Romans 3:20—"By the law is the knowledge of sin" (Rom 7:7).

2. It brings guilt and condemnation.
Romans 3:19—"Now we know that what things soever the law saith, it saith to them who are under the law: that every mouth may be stopped, and all the world may become guilty before God."

3. It acts as a spiritual mirror.
James 1:23-25—"If any be a hearer of the Word, and not a doer, he is like unto a man beholding his natural face in a glass: for he beholdeth himself, and goeth his way, and straightway forgetteth what manner of man he was. But whoso looketh into the perfect law of liberty, and continueth therein, he being not a forgetful hearer, but a doer of the work, this man shall be blessed in his deed" *(also James 2:9-12).*

Without the law, the sinner is like a man who is afflicted with a deadly disease that he doesn't know he has. Paul said, "I had not known sin, but by the law" (Rom 7:7).

9 - WHAT IS THE LAW UNABLE TO DO FOR THE SINNER?

The law cannot forgive. Law does not possess the power to forgive those who transgress its precepts. Only the Lawgiver can do that. Jesus died to redeem us from the curse of the law (Gal. 3:13). The law cannot keep the sinner from sinning because "the carnal mind is enmity against God: for it is not subject to the law of God, neither indeed can be" (Rom. 8:7).

The law only shows the sinner where he needs to change; but the law, itself, cannot change him. And so let us get three facts about the law very clear.

1. It cannot forgive or justify.
Romans 3:20—"By the deeds of the law there shall no flesh be justified in His sight."

2. It cannot keep from sin or sanctify.
Galatians 3:21—"Is the law then against the promises of God? God forbid: for if there had been a law given which could have given life, verily righteousness should have been by the law."

3. It cannot cleanse or keep the heart clean (Rom 9:3, 7-8).

The law is limited in its ability to do all that needs to be done for the sinner. A wound cannot be sewed up with only a needle. The thread of the gospel must do that.

10 - WHAT DOES THE GRACE OF CHRIST DO FOR THE SINNER?

When the law of God and the Spirit of God have made the sinner conscious of his sin, he will then feel his need of Christ and go to the Saviour for pardon. The publican found it so (Luke 18:13-14). The woman taken in adultery felt condemned and ashamed. She needed sympathy and forgiveness, and Christ was ready to grant these to her. Then He said, "Sin no more."

If we confess and put away sin, He will forgive (1 John 1:9). This is grace, or unmerited favor. This gracious love of Christ awakens love in the heart of the sinner, and he then desires to serve and obey God. Here are four elements of the saving grace of Christ:

1. It forgives and justifies.

Acts 13:38-39—"Be it known unto you therefore, men and brethren, that through this man is preached unto you the forgiveness of sins: and by Him all that believe are justified from all things, from which ye could not be justified by the law of Moses" (Luke 18:13-14).

2. It saves from sin, or sanctifies.

Matthew 1:21—"She shall bring forth a son, and thou shalt call His name Jesus: for He shall save His people from their sins."

1 Corinthians 1:30—"But of Him are ye in Christ Jesus, who of God is made unto us wisdom, and righteousness, and sanctification, and redemption."

3. It inspires faith.

Ephesians 2:8-10—"By grace are ye saved through faith; and that not of yourselves: it is the gift of God: not of works, lest any man should boast. For we are His workmanship, created in Christ Jesus unto good works, which God hath before ordained that we should walk in them."

4. It brings God's power.

Romans 1:16—"I am not ashamed of the gospel of Christ: for it is the power of God unto salvation to every one that believeth; to the Jew first, and also to the Greek."

Forgiveness of sin and power over sin come through the exercise of

Entering a Deeper Walk with God

simple faith in God's promises and a full surrender of the heart to Him.

11 - HOW DOES A SINNER SAVED BY GRACE RELATE TO THE LAW?

1. The law becomes the standard of his life.

1 John 5:3—"This is the love of God, that we keep His commandments."

2. He permits Christ to fulfill in him the righteousness of the law.

Romans 8:3-4—"God sending His own Son in the likeness of sinful flesh, and for sin, condemned sin in the flesh: that the righteousness of the law might be fulfilled in us, who walk not after the flesh, but after the Spirit."

3. Christ writes the law in his heart.

Hebrews 8:10—"This is the covenant that I will make with the house of Israel after those days, saith the Lord; I will put My laws into their mind, and write them in their hearts: and I will be to them a God, and they shall be to Me a people" (also Ps 119:11).

"Thou wilt keep him in perfect peace, whose mind is stayed on Thee: because He trusteth in Thee. Trust ye in the Lord for ever; for in the Lord Jehovah is everlasting strength."

—Isaiah 26:3-4

"The Lord is nigh unto them that are of a broken heart, and saveth such as be of a contrite spirit."

—Psalm 34:18

The most complete low-cost book—telling, in fascinating detail, the entire story of the Bible Sabbath—is *Beyond Pitcairn*. If you would like a copy of this 256-page book, in the U.S. send $5.00—and a postpaid copy will be rushed to you. Foreign, add US$6.00.

HARVESTIME BOOKS, BOX 300, ALTAMONT, TN 37301

Source Index

A

Acts of the Apostles, 291-292 43
Ambrose, Sermo vii. 13 33
Andrews, Samuel J., *The Life of Our Lord Upon the Earth*, 17 (New York: Charles Scribner's Sons, 1891) 19

B

Bede, *De temp. rat.*, ch. 13 33
Bible Commentary, Vol. 2, 1022 86
Bibiothica Sacra, Vol. 12, 153-155 42
Brady, Priest, in an address at Elizabeth, N.J., March 17, 1903; reported in the *Elizabeth N.J. News*, March 18, 1903 109
British Parliament *Act of 1644* 33
Buck, Charles, *Theological Dictionary*, "Christmas," 71 (Philadelphia: Crissy and Markley, copyright 1851) 19

C

Catholic Encyclopedia, 1911 ed., "Christmas." 6
Clarke, Adam, *Commentary*, Vol. 5, 370 5
Code of Justinian, Book 111, title 12, law 3 13
Constantine, *Edict of Milan* 13
Council of Trent, Session 13: *Decree on the Eucharist*, chap. 5 (Denz. 878, 1648) 41
Counsels on Health, 458 73
Cumont, Franz, *Astrology and Religion Among the Greeks and Romans* (reprint; New York: Dover Publications, Inc., 1960), 89-90 23
Cumont, Franz, *The Mysteries of Mithra*, Trans. by T.J. McCormack, 167, 191 22
Cyprian, *De orat. dom* 35) 33

D

De Pascha computus 32
Dickens, Charles, *A Christmas Carol* 35
Durant, Will, *History of Civilization*, Vol. 1, 127 54
Durant, Will, *History of Civilization*, Vol. 1, 235 54
Durant, Will, *History of Civilization*, Vol. 1, 238-239 54
Durant, Will, *History of Civilization*, Vol. 1, 296-297 53
Durant, Will, *History of Civilization*, Vol. 1, 372 57
Durant, Will, *History of Civilization*, Vol. 2, 178 55

E

Encyclopedia Americana (1944 edition), "Christmas." 7
Encyclopedia Britannica (1946 ed.) 8
Encyclopedia Britannica, Vol. VI, "Christmas," 293, 294, 11th edition 34
English Puritans 33
Enright, Priest Thomas, CSSR, President of Redemptorist

Source Index

College, Kansas City, MO, in a lecture at *Hartford, Kansas Weekly Call*, February 22, 1884, and the *American Sentinel* (a New York Roman Catholic journal), June 1893, 173 109

Episcopus Puerorum 31

Eusebius, Bishop of Caesarea, quoted in Commentary on the Psalms, in Migne, *Patrologia Graeca*, Vol. 23, Col. 1171 14

F

Fausset, A.R., *Bible Dictionary*, 666 9

G

Gibbon, Cardinal James, *The Faith of Our Fathers*, chapter 8 109

Grueber, H.A., *Myths of Northern Lands*, Vol. I (New York, 1895), 61 38

Great Controversy, 48 63

Great Controversy, 49-50 63

Great Controversy, 574 14

H

Haskins, Frederick J., *Answers to Questions* 40

Hippolytus, *Commentary*, "Daniel 4:23" (c. A.D. 202) 32

Hislop, Alexander, *The Two Babylons*, 7th edition, 92-94 26

Hyde, Walter Woodburn, *Paganism to Christianity in the Roman Empire*, 60 23

Hyde, Walter Woodburn, *Paganism to Christianity in the Roman Empire*, 249-250 18

I

Irving, Washington, *Sketch Book* 35

J

Justinian, *Code of*, Book 111, title 12, law 3 13

L

Laing, Gordon J., *Survivals of Roman Religion* (New York: Longmans, 1931), 150-153 22

Laing, Gordon J., *Survivals of Roman Religion* (New York: Longmans, 1931), 58, 62-65 31

Lamer, H., "Mithras," *Worterbuch der Antike*, 2nd ed. (Leipzig: A. Kroner, 1933) 22

Langdon, Stephen H., "Semitic Mythology," in *The Mythology of All Races*, Vol. 5 (Boston: Archaeological Institute of America, Marshall Jones Company, 1931), 15-19 28

Lange, John P., *Church History*, Vol. 2, 395 (N.Y.) 28

Lange, John Peter, *Commentary on the Holy Scriptures*, "Luke 2:36 (New York: Charles Scribner & Co., 1870) 29

M

Magdeburg Centuriators (i. 3, 118) 31

Migne, *Patrologia Graeca*, Vol. 23, Col. 1171 14

Mommsen 32

N

Newman, A.H, "Christmas," *New Scaff-Herzog Encyclopedia of Religious Knowledge*, Vol. 3, 47 18

Newman, A.H, "Christmas," *New Scaff-Herzog Encyclopedia of Religious Knowledge* 6

O

Origen, "Eighth Homily on Leviticus" 32

Origen, quoted in *Catholic Encyclopedia,* "Natal Day." 11th ed. 6

P

Parliament, *Act of 1644* 33

Patriarchs and Prophets, 684-685 73

Polycarp 33

Pope Gregory III (A.D. 731-741) 65

Pope Gregory IV (827-844) 65

Pope Leo XIII, Encyclical Letter, June 20, 1894; *The Great Encyclical Letters of Leo XIII,* p. 304 109

S

Segur, Monsignor Louis, *Plain Talk About the Protestantism of Today,* 213 113

Smith, Albert, Chancellor of the Archdiocese of Baltimore, letter dated February 10, 1920 (Replying for Cardinal Gibbons) 109

Southern Publishing Association, "Easter: Where It Came From" 44

Sozomen, quoted in *Ecclesiastical History,* book 7, chapter 19; now in *A Select Library of Nicene and Post-Nicene Fathers,* second series, Vol. 2 15

Steps to Christ, 51 to 111 (abridged) 100

Steps to Christ, 9-51 (abridged) 92

Strom., i. 21 17

T

Theophilus of Antioch 31

Thomas, H.F., writing for Cardinal James Gibbons, November 11, 1895 110

V

Vatican II: *The Conciliar and Post Conciliar Documents* 41

von Mosheim, John Laurence, *Institutes of Ecclesiastical History,* book 2, cent. 4, part 2, chap. 4, sec. 5 (Vol. I, 372-373). London: Longman & Co., 1841 19

W

World Book, Vol. 1, 782 52

Weiser, Francis X., *Handbook of Christian Feasts and Customs* (New York: Harcourt, Brace and World, Inc., 1958), 60-62 21

Weiser, Francis X., *Handbook of Christian Feasts and Customs* (New York: Harcourt, Brace and World, Inc., 1958), 60-62 36

Weiser, Francis X., *Handbook of Christian Feasts and Customs* (New York: Harcourt, Brace and World, Inc., 1958), 103-104 39

Weiser, Francis X., *Handbook of Christian Feasts and Customs* (New York: Harcourt, Brace and World, Inc., 1958), 113-114 38

Weiser, Francis X., *Handbook of Christian Feasts and Customs,* 312-313 71

Weiser, Francis X., *Handbook of Christian Feasts and Customs* (New York: Harcourt, Brace and World, Inc., 1958), 315-316 70

For More Information

GREAT CONTROVERSY—The story is traced so vividly that this volume has become one of the most widely distributed best sellers of modern times, with editions in a score of languages. 448 pp.

MINISTRY OF HEALING—Health of body, healing of disease, peace of heart - through simple, natural remedies combined with trust in divine power. 360 pp.

DESIRE OF AGES—The gripping story of Christ's life, from the manger to Calvary - and how it can help your life today. 856 pp.

BIBLE READINGS—180 chapters in 18 sections make this an outstanding Bible study aid. Outstanding value. Easy-to-read print size, plus 3 indexes - and all at an easy-to-buy price. 648 pp.

CHRIST'S OBJECT LESSONS—All the wonderful parables of Jesus, the Master Teacher. How to live better now - and how to prepare for an eternity with Him afterward. 376 pp.

SHELTER IN THE STORM—An outstanding handbook on Christian living; one you will come to value. All the steps to Christ are carefully explained, plus much more. 216 pp.

BEYOND PITCAIRN—A fascinating journey to other lands - that will finally bring you into the heart of one of history's strangest mysteries. 256 pp.

MARK OF THE BEAST—Part 1 explains the Mark in Daniel 7 and Revelation 12-14. Dozens of facts and statements from historical sources. Part 2 is word-for-word from the heart of *Great Controversy*. 208 pp.

NATIONAL SUNDAY LAW CRISIS—The history of the Sunday law movement in America and where it is leading us. A powerful book, with a full chapter on the implications of the Genocide Treaty. 112 pp.

YOU CAN QUIT TOBACCO—Careful step-by-step information about why you must quit and how to do it. This has helped many people. 104 pp.

DEFENDING GOD—God did not create a devil. He does not cause our sufferings. He does not torture people when they die. The truth about hellfire. 176 pp.

EVOLUTION CRUNCHER—Thousands of scientific facts, disproving every basic area of evolutionary theory. A fascinating book that is easy to read. 1350 scientific quotations or references. Written for all ages. 928 pp.

The worship of Mithra, the dying-rising Sun god who returns to life each December 25.
 —*Later being transformed into the "Christ mass" celebration.*

The worship of Ishtar, the goddess of love and licentiousness, and her god son, Tammuz, who is resurrected each spring.
 —*Later becoming the "Easter" celebration.*

The worship of black cats, ghosts, bonfires, witches, demons, and the dead on the eve before Hallows Day, each October 31.
 —*Later adopting the form of the "Halloween" celebration.*

Bible Treasures –

Would you like to understand your Bible better? Eternal treasures are contained within it. Simply fill out and mail the following slip. Entirely free, with no obligation.

NAME ....

ADDRESS ....

STATE .... ZIP ....

SEND TO: HARVESTIME BOOKS - ALTAMONT, TN 37301

For additional literature, please contact the address below: